THE USUAL SUSPECTS

Karl Keating

THE USUAL SUSPECTS

Answering Anti-Catholic Fundamentalists

IGNATIUS PRESS   SAN FRANCISCO

Cover design by Roxanne Mei Lum

© 2000 Ignatius Press, San Francisco
All rights reserved

ISBN 0–89870–773–0
Library of Congress catalogue number 99–75400

Printed in the United States of America ⊗

For Justin

CONTENTS

PREFACE

This book is not so much a sequel as a supplement to *Catholicism and Fundamentalism*. In that book I tried to give a panoramic view of the attack on "Romanism" by "Bible Christians", highlighting prominent anti-Catholic individuals and organizations and discussing at length controverted doctrines. Here I present snapshots, individualized portraits—some larger, some smaller—of arguments and people opposed to the Catholic faith.

The first eight chapters give an overview, from several different angles. The second eight recount attacks and confusions that may strain credulity but still fall within the realm of civil discourse. The third eight feature journeys into the bizarre. I draw things to a close with reviews of two video productions.

Determining which chapters should fall into which sections was not easy. Readers who think some chapters ought to swap places will not receive a complaint from me. *De gustibus non est disputandum.*

PART ONE

Advice and Dissent

I

The Roman System Way

A subscriber to the magazine I used to edit wrote to tell me she did not need answers from Catholics any longer:

> God's Word, the Bible, has become exactly that to me! I've found without a doubt his Word is all I need! He causes me to grow as I study it and sit under good Bible preaching where everyone brings a Bible to follow along as he compares Scripture to Scripture! When I accepted the Lord Jesus as my personal Lord and Savior, I had no intention of leaving "Holy Mother the Church"—in fact, I thought *now* I'll be like the others and know the what, where, and why of it all. . . . And then I started listening to the priest at Mass, and I could see I would have to choose one or the other: the Bible way or the Roman system way. The answer is obvious. Then, when I got together with the parish priest, he told me I was too fanatic about the Bible! I replied, "Thank you for the compliment." What more did I need? . . . No more literature, please.

Reading between the lines, you can imagine what happened. The story is a common one. This woman found no intellectual fulfillment at her parish. Probably, like many parishes, it was just coasting, and she was a once-a-week Catholic. Then a Protestant friend invited her to a service at the neighborhood born-again church. At first my correspondent

put her off. Going seemed a bit disloyal, and what did Bible
thumpers have to offer anyway? (All she knew about born-
agains she had gathered from reruns of *Elmer Gantry*.)

But her friend kept pestering her, in a gentle way, and
finally she consented. I'll sit through it once, she thought,
and that will be it. Well, it certainly was it—it was just what
she was looking for. She discovered "good Bible preaching".
Here was a minister who spoke her language, convicted her
of sin, and seemed to have the Bible memorized. He was at
once blunt in condemnation of the easy, quasi-Christian life
she had been living and had been satisfied with (more or less)
and encouraging in his eagerness that Christianity be extended to all. What is more, he did not look or sound like
Elmer Gantry. He did not wear polyester or a leisure suit, and
he did not wear expensive suits either. He did not look like a
huckster, a nerd, or a con artist. He had a soothing voice and
could speak (how to describe it?) not professionally (he was
not polished or slick) but honestly, from the heart. He would
not be mistaken for a scholar, but he clearly was a believer.
And he was friendly. After the service her friend introduced
her to the minister, and he introduced her to others at the
small church. At her home parish there was a rigorous ano-
nymity. You could attend for years and be recognized as a
regular, but no one would know your name. Here, at this
small church, everyone seemed to know everyone.

That is how it all started. She was invited to join a Bible
study class. Why not? she thought. She dusted off the family
Bible and went, but soon put that Bible aside and purchased a
King James Version so she could read along with the others.
She was surprised to find she enjoyed reading the Bible, and
she read it often. At the Bible study she at first bristled when
people said the Bible supported this or that doctrine—doctrines opposed to what the Catholic Church taught. It was

not that they bad-mouthed Catholicism as such. Actually, Catholicism hardly ever came up. Instead, it was pointed out to her that peculiarly Protestant doctrines were true, and by implication peculiarly Catholic ones were not.

She read, for instance, about the "brethren of the Lord". She always had thought these were Jesus' cousins, but everyone at the Bible study insisted they were his brothers-german. What they said seemed to make sense. At least she did not have anything to say on behalf of the Catholic position. (Of course, she did not really know what the Catholic position was based on, so she should have expected it to seem inadequate.)

So it went. Week after week she attended both Mass and the Protestant service, and she joined in the Bible study. She became convinced that everything to be believed must be found plainly on the face of the Bible. The Bible was written for simple people, she was told, so there could not be a need to draw out tendentious inferences. She realized, after a while, that she was happier attending the Bible study or the Protestant service than attending Mass. The priest did not have much to say anyhow, just a lot of banal comments about political issues in which she took no interest (never—to her, a telling point—any comments about sin).

Then came the hard sell, though she did not see it as such. Her new friends explained that Catholicism is not really Christianity as Christ intended it. Instead, it is a religious *system*. That means it is a scheme through which you effect your own salvation by doing things: going to Mass, taking Communion, going to confession, getting indulgences, praying to statues, and so on. You either choose the Bible way or the Roman system way, she was told.

By this time she knew where her affections lay—she simply liked the Protestants more than the Catholics, the minister more than the priest—and it seemed her beliefs were moving in the same direction as her feelings. She thought she would give the Catholic Church one last chance. She made an appointment to see her pastor and was not surprised that he did not even know her name, though she had been in the parish for years. She explained to him her devotion to the Bible and how, so far as she could see, all Christian truths are to be found in the Bible and anything not obviously in the Bible is to be rejected. It's the Bible or nothing, she said. If the Bible is true, it couldn't be incomplete. There couldn't be a need for anything else. Now, what do you have to say to *that*, Father?

He said something about her putting a wrong emphasis on the Bible, about not having a right appreciation of Christianity and its history. What he meant, she thought, was that she was a fanatic. It had to seem so to him—after all, *he* never preached from the Bible. Maybe he never even read it, except for those readings at Mass.

Their meeting was short. He was in a hurry, and she was uncomfortable. When she got home she knew what she had to do. It was like when her husband died. After a while, she gathered up things that reminded her of him and threw them away. She did the same with things that reminded her of Catholicism. Gone from the wall was the crucifix, to the trash went the pamphlets and books she had accumulated (not many, and mostly unread), and the rosary she hid in the attic, along with the Catholic Bible. She wrote a few letters, telling people "no more literature, please". And that was that.

Such is my reconstruction of what is behind the letter. Decide for yourself whether it is a likely scenario. What is sure is that it is a common one. Not that I get many letters like this woman's—in fact, hers was the first ever from a subscriber who was bidding a fond farewell to Rome—but what she went through many people go through. Notice the progression. It begins with dissatisfaction at the parish. The practice of one's faith is nothing more than a once-a-week thing: leave home for Mass, back within an hour. Then comes an invitation to visit an Evangelical or Fundamentalist church. At first the invitation is declined; eventually it is accepted: "just this one time". The friendliness of the congregation and the speaking skills of the preacher seem impressive compared to what is found at Mass, where few parishioners know one another, where the priest seems to do his best (and, too often, succeeds) in trivializing the liturgy.

So the first impression of Evangelicalism or Fundamentalism is of Evangelicals or Fundamentalists, and the impression is positive. There is a certain attraction, and it is all at the emotional level. The Catholic is willing to let himself be indoctrinated—in the good sense of having doctrine poured into him, not in the bad sense of being brainwashed—and he is a little surprised to discover the new doctrines taking hold. He should not be. They are being poured into a vacuum. They do not have to displace by force of logic any preexisting doctrines, because what Catholic doctrines already are there are held only at a juvenile level. The Catholic never was catechized as an adult, and his sixth-grade understandings are pushed aside easily by the new doctrines he is meeting now.

That is the positive side of indoctrination. The negative consists of arguments against Catholicism. The Catholic—now half Catholic, half Protestant—has no intellectual defenses. He has nothing to say. He is not browbeaten into accepting conclusions that are unflattering to Catholicism—what can he do *but* accept them, since he has never heard any explanation or defense of the Catholic side? Yes, along the way he swallows a lot of unclear thinking and even some outright nonsense, but not consciously. It all seems to fit together.

So he finds himself making that one last trip to the rectory. For many people who leave the Church, it is both the first and last time they speak with a priest. The priest, as often as not, does not appreciate the stakes. He does not know it is make or break. This is not always the case, of course. There are many priests who are on their toes, who see what is coming and say all the right things, bringing their inquirers back into the faith. There are others who do not, usually because they do not see the warning signs, sometimes because they do but just do not care.

When the waverer leaves the rectory, he may be a waverer no longer. His worst suspicions may be confirmed ("Good Lord! That priest doesn't know anything about the Bible!"), and he quietly slips away. He makes no fuss, carries no picket signs. He just stops going to Mass and turns all his attention to his new faith.

2

The Only Game in Town

As recently as the early 1980s, anti-Catholicism was thought to be dead in the United States. Most pundits attributed its demise to John F. Kennedy's campaign pledge, made before Protestant ministers in Texas, that he would not let his Catholicism influence his decisions as president. But anti-Catholicism already had been on the wane for a generation. Its gradual disappearance coincided with the lessening influence of Fundamentalism and Evangelicalism, which met the social gospel in battle during the first decades of the century—and lost. When the social gospel later dissolved into secularism with a religious face, people again turned to Fundamentalist and Evangelical churches because they seemed to be the only ones willing to proclaim that doctrinal truth matters. Except in the South, where there have never been many Catholics, it is common to find that as many as half the congregants of these churches got where they are by "unpoping". This perhaps explains why many professional anti-Catholics—those who actually make a living at it—were once loyal to Rome. But not all. For every Bartholomew Brewer—former Carmelite priest and now Baptist minister and head of Mission to Catholics International—there is a Bob Jones, latest in a line of well-known anti-Catholics and head of a private university that bears his and his forebears' name.

The techniques vary widely. Jack Chick, one of those curiosities for which Southern California is famous, distributes in large quantities comic books depicting Romish intrigues as revealed by a man who claims to have been a Jesuit assigned to subvert Protestantism. These comics have received a lot of play in the Catholic press, but they are far less influential than other anti-Catholic material. They are so grotesque in their charges that even other opponents of the Church have written against their use.

The most effective propaganda confronts Catholics, and those who would be suspicious of Catholicism, with questions that seem to be damning. They seem so because American Catholics are remarkably ignorant of their faith and are baffled by even the simplest questions. (This will not surprise anyone who has taught a class of teen-aged confirmands and found that not one knew the Our Father, even though it is prayed at each Sunday Mass.) When Catholics go to their priests for answers to these questions, as often as not they come away disillusioned. Instead of frank and reasonable replies, they are given lame excuses, such as "because that's what we believe", or, worse, are told that "the Church no longer believes that anyway." One hardly can blame people for leaving a Church whose pastors are unable to resolve problems that in fact have straightforward and satisfying solutions.

It is these questions that are swelling Fundamentalist and Evangelical ranks across America. People in the pews are hungry for doctrinal truth. They have been brought up on scientific dogmas and expect yes-or-no answers in religion also. They are seeking answers that are more satisfying than the attitude that insists that it is not polite to talk about religion at cocktail parties or in church.

How many Catholics have left Saint Miscellanius' for Good

Book Baptist? It is hard to say. Some televangelists claim that more than a third of their viewers (and therefore contributors) are Catholics, and many of those Catholics are gradually disengaging themselves from Rome. Newsletters from anti-Catholic organizations are full of testimonials from people who have seen the light and who have been successful in coaxing their friends to join the exodus. A rough figure? Certainly several hundreds of thousands over the last decade and perhaps several million. Although there are said to be more than sixty million Catholics in the United States, many do not practice the faith and are Catholics only in the cultural sense. True, most of the dropouts in recent years have dropped into indifference, not Bible-thumpery, but there is a growing disenchantment with the lack of moorings even among the indifferent, and the tract pushers are making considerable headway. No annual reports are issued by the anti-Catholic groups, so it is hard to say just how many publications their presses turn out, but the number is surely in the multiple millions.

So far there seems to be little appreciation at the higher levels of the Church in America that something is going on that should serve as a lesson. There is a real need being met by Fundamentalists and Evangelicals; they are not simply better than Catholics at glad-handing. The key is that they are talking about doctrines. That they are confused on doctrinal matters is not the point. The point is that, given the lethargy of the Church here, to many Americans they are looking like the only game in town.

3

How Evangelicals Handle Cults

If you visit a "Christian" bookstore—that is, one with books appealing mainly to Evangelicals and Fundamentalists—you will find several shelves given over to works debunking the cults. When conservative Protestants use the word "cult", they do not have in mind such things as the cult of a saint. They mean instead religions, more or less removed in appearance from Christianity, that provide believers with, not merely a set of doctrines, but social and emotional support so intense that the believers are disinclined to question their doctrines. Some Fundamentalists go so far as to claim Catholicism is a cult, but this is a minority viewpoint. Most Fundamentalists say Catholicism is not a cult—it is just wrong.

But this is not about attitudes toward Catholicism. It is about what Catholics can learn from Protestants who write against cults. Consider one writer in particular: Anthony A. Hoekema, a professor of systematic theology, a Calvinist, and the author of *The Four Major Cults*. The religions Hoekema examines are Mormonism, Seventh-Day Adventism, Christian Science, and Jehovah's Witnesses. The final chapter of his book is called "Approaching the Cultist", and it is his recommendations that are examined here.

(By the way: I reproduce Hoekema's use of the words

"cult" and "cultist", even though their use might strike Catholics as sometimes uncharitable, sometimes improper. I use them merely out of convenience, so that my language will parallel Hoekema's. Normally I do not use the terms when discussing what William Whalen, a Catholic writer, terms "minority religions".[1] These terms have a pejorative ring to them and encourage finger-pointing. All some people need to do, to write off a religion, is to label it a cult. Catholics have been at the receiving end of such labeling and should be careful about taking up such loaded words.)

The first subsection of Hoekema's last chapter is about "difficulties". The problems are several, he says. "To begin with, the cultist is not a religiously indifferent person; he is 'deeply religious' to the point of fanaticism. Having rejected historic Christianity, he can be counted on to be antagonistic to the testimony of a Christian believer."[2] What's more, "the cultist firmly believes he has found the truth, and hence he considers the message of historic Christianity to be inferior to the doctrines he has obtained through 'special revelation' or through some inspired channel of truth."[3] The cultist is a victim of a "kind of mass delusion of grandeur, coupled with a great deal of pride". He has had "to endure considerable ridicule from his kith and kin since joining the cult and is even now sacrificing much of his time and effort in making propaganda for the group. Hence it is not going to be easy to induce him to leave the cult."[4]

Hoekema points out, rightly, that "the mere reading of a pamphlet or brochure on a particular cult does not qualify

---

[1] William J. Whalen, *Minority Religions in America* (New York: Alba House, 1972).

[2] Anthony A. Hoekema, *The Four Major Cults* (Grand Rapids, Mich.: Eerdmans, 1963), 405.

[3] Ibid.

[4] Ibid., 406.

one for conducting a thoroughgoing polemic against the cult."[5] (The same can be said about those who base their opposition to Catholicism on "the mere reading of a pamphlet or brochure".) To speak with a cultist intelligently, one must be well grounded in the cult's doctrines and in Scripture, says Hoekema. He mentions a woman who had been a Jehovah's Witness. Going door to door, she

> encountered three types of responses. Some slammed doors in her face. These people made her feel good, since their action was construed as persecution for the sake of her faith. A second group of people argued heatedly and belligerently. These only strengthened her convictions, since she had ready answers for their arguments. A third group gave her a personal testimony of their faith in Christ. These, so she said, made the most lasting impression on her; when she went to bed at night, she would think about these people and reflect on what they had said. Surely every true believer ought to be able to give this kind of testimony.[6]

And a few true believers should do more, he says. They should make a concerted study of a cult in order to give a Christian response to it.

Before moving on, notice, for a moment, what this woman *did not* report. She did not report a fourth group: people who argued with her coolly and charitably. The only arguments she got were heated and belligerent. However important personal testimony is, it is not enough. We need to use our brains, not only our hearts. (Yet keep in mind that Catholics, too often trained to think intellectual banter is enough to effect a conversion, often underestimate the power of a personal testimony.) If this woman had encountered a Catholic who not only could testify to what his faith had done for him

---

[5] Ibid.
[6] Ibid., 406–7.

but could explain what the Church really teaches, she might have come all the way to the fullness of Christian faith that is found at Rome.

Hoekema says that the Christian evangelist—he has in mind conservative Protestants—must approach the cultist as a "total person". He means that one should not see the cultist "just as someone whose doctrines need to be refuted but as someone whom we love, about whom we are concerned in the totality of his life. We should therefore try to find out, if we can, why he joined this cult. Did he previously belong to a church? If so, why did he leave it? What shortcomings did he find in it? In what way did the church fail to satisfy his needs? What benefits is he deriving from membership in the group to which he now belongs? What does this group do for him that the church failed to do?"[7]

Much of the attraction of the cults, says Hoekema, is at the social rather than the doctrinal level, but he does not forget that a person would not stay in a cult if he did not accept its beliefs. You can do without emotional support, at least for a while; you cannot do without intellectual support. When you cease to believe what the cult teaches, you jump ship, no matter how friendly your fellow cultists might be.

Hoekema then comes up with the Big Question: "Right at this point the cultist should be asked, Do you have complete assurance of salvation?"[8] Unlike many Evangelicals and Fundamentalists (but by no means all), the Jehovah's Witness, the Mormon, and the Seventh-Day Adventist (and the Catholic, for that matter) will say, "No." "Over against this uncertainty we must place the granite certainty of the Christian faith", says Hoekema.[9] He takes as a given that one can

---

[7] Ibid., 409.
[8] Ibid., 410.
[9] Ibid.

have an absolute assurance of salvation, and he does not seem to realize that this is, historically, a novel position. It can be traced no farther back than the Reformation. It is not the ancient Christian—which is to say, Catholic—position. Here, as elsewhere, Hoekema offers a second-best approach to the cultist. He cannot offer anything more because his is a second-best position itself.

The next subsection of this final chapter is called "Approaching the Cultist on the Intellectual Level". Hoekema gives several "general suggestions", followed by several "specific suggestions".[10] "We must approach the cultist with genuine love. Though we may never love his errors, we must love him as a person."[11] Good counsel, very difficult to follow. Most of us have trouble distinguishing the believer from the belief, the sinner from the sin, the nut from the nuttiness, but we have to do our best.

We should understand, says Hoekema, that "our primary purpose, however, may never be to defeat the cultist in argument or to demolish his position, but to win him for Christ."[12] He goes on to say—tellingly—that "the cultist has been taught that the members of regular churches regard him with hostility; the most effective way to disabuse him of that notion is to reveal a loving concern quite different from what he has been led to expect. This implies, needless to say, that we must never lose our tempers during the encounter but must remain calm and self-controlled."[13]

This has been brought home to me through experience. At parish seminars and debates, I try to keep my frustrations to myself. Sometimes non-Catholic listeners are hostile,

[10] Ibid., 412–16.
[11] Ibid., 412.
[12] Ibid.
[13] Ibid.

sometimes disruptive, sometimes rude. The urge to give as one has received can be almost overpowering, but so far I do not think I have thrown any wicked one-liners, the kind that cut to the heart more effectively than any stiletto. The restraint has paid off. After many public appearances, Protestants thank me for speaking well of their position and for not getting riled. Many want to find out more about the Catholic faith. How many of them would have gone away with their worst suspicions confirmed if I had used against their beliefs the kind of language used against mine by professional anti-Catholics? How many Catholics would have been scandalized and would have found themselves distancing themselves from the Church instead of embracing her ever more closely?

Hoekema goes on to say that "we should approach the cultist with humility. We can be on the right side yet be incapable of representing it rightly. We can know the truth yet not pass it along intelligibly. We can assume rashly that right knowing necessarily implies able teaching, but we have to work at learning to teach. Such skill doesn't come automatically." Then, he says, "we must know the teachings of the cult." [14] The trick is in being fair to those teachings. The temptation is so to simplify them that they become caricatures. If the cultist will not recognize his faith in our description of it, how can we expect him to be moved by what we then say about it?

Next come Hoekema's specific suggestions. It is here that the Catholic reader will find the greatest weaknesses.

"Face the question of your source of authority", insists Hoekema. "If you are talking to a Mormon, you must first show him from the Bible, which he does recognize as a

---

[14] Ibid., 412–13.

sacred book, that Scripture itself teaches its own sufficiency
and condemns the attempt to add other sources of revelation
to it." [15] There are two problems here. The Mormon has an
out. He realizes the Book of Mormon does not square with
the Bible. His solution is simple: "The Bible has been mis-
translated wherever it contradicts the Book of Mormon." If
he works from that premise, no listing of contradictions will
convince him of the spuriousness of the Book of Mormon.
That is one problem. The other is a problem with Hoekema's
own position. The fact is that the Bible nowhere claims to be
sufficient as a rule of faith. Paul writes that it is "profitable",
not sufficient (2 Tim 3:16). Coming from a Reformed position, Hoekema naturally dismisses Tradition, in the proper
Catholic sense, as being nonexistent. He can see only "traditions of men". Notice his reference to "other sources of
revelation". In Hoekema's mind these sources include the
Book of Mormon, the writings of Mary Baker Eddy and
Ellen G. White, and Catholic Tradition.

Even though the Bible is not the sole rule of faith, much
good can come from comparing what it says with what these
other religions teach. This is especially true when one speaks
with Jehovah's Witnesses, since they do not recognize as
inspired any books other than the Bible. (Christian Scientists
say they do not regard Mrs. Eddy's writings as inspired, and
Adventists say the same about Mrs. White's writings, but
in practice these works are often put nearly on a par with
Scripture.)

Hoekema says the Christian should "present the evidence
for the major doctrines of the Christian faith".[16] He immediately runs into a conundrum. Which doctrines are these?
Not the ones that "set your denomination apart from other

[15] Ibid., 414.
[16] Ibid., 415.

Christian denominations", but the doctrines "which are held in common by all Evangelical Christians".[17] Unfortunately, if that is what is to be presented, a kind of "mere Evangelical Christianity", then there will not be much to be said. The sad fact is that even Evangelicals are divided on doctrine. A faith built only on those few doctrines on which they all agree would be a thin, unsatisfying faith: little sustenance for a child, not remotely enough for an adult.

"Stick to the major doctrines", says Hoekema. "Do not allow yourself to be sidetracked into discussing minor issues." [18] What is a minor issue for one man may be a major issue for another. There are any number of people whose problems with respect to Catholicism can be reduced to a single issue—and that issue a minor one. If it is not dealt with, no progress can be made. Infant baptism is not among your top ten issues, you say? It is for some people. For some this issue must be resolved before any further illumination is possible. If you sidestep infant baptism when it is brought up, claiming it is too insignificant for notice, some minds will close.

Hoekema always counsels "direct appeal to Scripture".[19] This is important but not always adequate. On many things Scripture speaks with an unclear voice or is entirely silent. You have to look elsewhere for support. One good place is early Christian history, including the history of dogmas and the history of practices or customs. Through such history we discover what early Christians believed, and we may infer from their belief what the apostles taught. Did Ignatius of Antioch believe in a hierarchy and the Real Presence? Then we may conclude he was taught them by John the Evangelist,

[17] Ibid.
[18] Ibid.
[19] Ibid.

whose student he was, and John, of course, learned directly from the Messiah.

The last two admonitions made by Hoekema are worth remembering: "Follow up the contact made", and "Keep on praying." [20] A single conversation is almost never enough to effect a conversion, and no number of conversations, no amount of instruction, will work without prayer. These are good points from a Protestant writer from whom a Catholic can learn much, even while disagreeing on much.

[20] Ibid., 416.

4

Argument by Sneer

Maybe Jerry Falwell was off his feed. When the manuscript for *Fundamentalism Today: What Makes It So Attractive?* came across his desk, he may have had time only for skimming. He may not have appreciated how deeply unfair these collected essays are to Fundamentalism. Or maybe he did. Maybe he read them carefully and decided a caveat to the reader might do some good. He might have said to himself, "Yes, I'll agree to write a foreword; it may let prospective readers know this book is a crock."

At any rate, Falwell's short foreword is the most balanced part of this book. The most unbalanced may be the contribution by Robert W. Shinn, professor of religion and philosophy at Eastern College in Pennsylvania. The thesis of his essay is that Fundamentalism (and, by implication, orthodox Christianity of any persuasion, including the Catholic) is low on the scale of religious maturity. Shinn recounts and gladly accepts the ideas of James Fowler, who wrote *Stages of Faith: The Psychology of Human Development and the Quest for Meaning*. Fowler, a Methodist minister, relied heavily on the ideas of Lawrence Kohlberg, famous for his thesis that there are stages of moral maturity, with liberals like Kohlberg near the top, believers in the Ten Commandments toward the bottom. What Kohlberg did for morality, Fowler did for religion, and Shinn proposes to tell us about it.

He begins by noting that, "according to Fowler, faith is an innate primal response and trust in ultimate reality."[1] This definition of faith has nothing to do with the Christian notion, of course, whether Protestant or Catholic. The Protestant's fiduciary faith and the Catholic's confessional faith are quite distinct. Shinn, with Fowler, notes that "all of us grow morally, socially, and educationally in different ways and at different rates. Can it be that the religious dimension is exempt from this growth process?" Of course not. Six stages can be identified, it is said, and here they are:

Stage one: Intuitive-projective (ages four to eight): Here we see the "rise of imagination" and the "formation of images of the numinous and an ultimate environment".[2]

Stage two: Mythical-literal (ages eight to twelve): This is characterized by "the rise of narrative and the forming of stories of faith".[3]

Stage three: Synthetic-conventional (from puberty onward, "sometimes for a lifetime"): The key here is "the forming of identity and the shaping of personal faith".[4] This is the level at which most Fundamentalists find themselves; by implication, the average Catholic is here too. Note the disparaging "conventional": What Joe Average believes is conventional; what university professors believe, even if they march in lockstep, is not.

Stage four: Individual-reflective (late teens to middle age): This level features the "reflective construction of an ideol-

[1] Robert W. Shinn, "Fundamentalism as a Case of Arrested Development", in *Fundamentalism Today: What Makes It So Attractive?*, ed. Marla J. Selvidge (Elgin, Ill.: Brethren Press, 1984), 91.

[2] Ibid.

[3] Ibid.

[4] Ibid., 92.

ogy" and the "formation of a vocational dream".[5] You can sense by the phrasing that this level, like the previous one, is for the hoi polloi.

Stage five: Paradoxical-consolidative ("midlife and beyond"): Here we get to "paradox, depth, recognition of mystery, and responsibility for the world".[6] The religious liberal, whose faith may be reduced to social action, feels at home here.

Stage six: Universalist ("occasionally with maturity"): "A state reached by rare individuals who identify with humanity with exceptional sensitivity".[7] Shinn and Fowler, with due modesty, do not seem to put themselves in stage six, being content, apparently, with the previous level.

What of Fundamentalists? "Fundamentalism manifests characteristics of stage 3. In a more enlightened form or phase, commonly called Evangelicalism, it manifests a few of the characteristics of stage 4."[8]

It should be said in his defense that Shinn notes that these stages are not clear divisions. "Characteristics from different stages can co-exist in any stage. Sometimes people are caught in a very prolonged transition between stages, thereby defying classification."[9] Not to worry. For the most part, we can pigeonhole people easily, particularly folks whose beliefs we do not like.

In stage three "adolescents reach out to 'find themselves' and interpret their lives through others in the community, such as those in their peer group, school, or vocation." "Childhood images of God may deepen through some experience or a distinct conversion. Children may find the God

[5] Ibid.
[6] Ibid.
[7] Ibid.
[8] Ibid.
[9] Ibid.

who knows and accepts them. As the adolescent participates in society, his fervent religiosity finds expression in a system of beliefs and values from a church, synagogue, youth organization, or Bible club. This is the stage at which foundations can be laid for continued growth. The traditions of believing groups can become real, and individuals can think for themselves." But many never do think for themselves, says Shinn. "There are both youths and adults who are satisfied with a system that answers most or all of their questions and provides the satisfaction of an 'in-group' that screens all 'reality' for them. Association with a group can be a good experience. The strength orthodoxy provides is a cohesive force in any group." [10]

One can agree with this to a certain extent, but Christianity is reduced to psychology. You are a Christian because you cannot stand on your own. You cannot face "real" reality, so you need a group to manufacture a different reality for you. "With stage 4 people shift from relying on conventional authorities to taking personal responsibility for their commitments, lifestyle, beliefs, and attitudes." [11] It is hard to escape the sense that this implies our religious maturity can be measured by the extent to which we form our faith in our own likeness.

What about religious authority? Shinn explains that "in stage 2 the Holy Bible is a very special book, God's Book, Mother's Book." (Mother's Book?) "Children can be in awe of it as a household fetish. In stage 3 the Bible is an authority that provides God's truth. At a naïve level the Bible and all its contents are sacred. . . . Therefore, you honor the Bible and God. At a more sophisticated level the Bible is the authority for conduct and belief. It is infallible or inerrant." [12] Catholics

[10] Ibid., 93
[11] Ibid.
[12] Ibid., 94.

disagree with Fundamentalists about the status of the Bible—
we do not believe in *sola scriptura*—but we can sympathize
with Fundamentalists whose religion is being travestied here.
We are only halfway up the ladder, and already we are on the
verge of dropping the Bible as an authority.

A story Shinn relates is revealing. He tells of a professor
who, "in a public lecture at Eastern College, reminisced
somewhat bitterly about a very early period in her life when
she had been indoctrinated by an ultra-conservative Protestant sect, a wing of the Plymouth Brethren. Her perception
of reality was to words and expressions taken directly from
the King James Bible and enforced as God's very words.
Everything was screened through this verbiage, she said,
and it took her years to get free of it. Stage 2 was preventing
the growth of even a systematic theology characteristic of
stage 3." But was liberation to be found? Yes, thank God.
"Having wrestled with feminist theology and the study of the
nature of God's attributes"—that is, having discovered he is a
she—the professor "testifies to her recognition and appreciation of divine mystery in relation to the finitude of all human
systems and language patterns." [13] That means she now believes we cannot know anything definite about God, so creeds
are a waste of time. This is how Shinn characterizes this
version of the Pilgrim's Progress: "What a testimony to the
sobering influence of a stage 5 transcendence of any and all
neatly packaged systems that limit openness to all aspects of a
given subject." [14] There seems to be, for Shinn and for his
mentor, Fowler, a definite correlation between disbelief and
religious maturity. Traditional Christians can be such only
because they have not advanced very far; people who have
left Christianity behind are on the road to nirvana.

[13] Ibid., 94–95.
[14] Ibid., 95.

Shinn feels a bit sorry for people stuck in stage four. Such "interpreters of the Bible may have to give lip service to creedal, institutional statements about infallibility or inerrancy that are officially binding upon them. Such statements of faith are often linked to seminaries, colleges, or denominations, but scholars in these institutions engage in historical-critical studies that if consistently pursued could cause them to march off the map of rigid, orthodox formulations of the nature and authority of the Bible. . . . For stage 3 conservatives such freedom of inquiry is dangerous indeed." [15] The reader is being told, and none too subtly, that truth is to be found among college instructors of a properly liberated bent. The Catholic reader is told, if he reads between the lines, that it is a good thing not to give anything more than "lip service to creedal" statements.

There is another problem here, says Shinn. Stage-three thinking, even stage-four thinking, is intellectually dishonest. If you are a thinker at all and stay at these levels, you are just faking it.

> A stage 5 friend of mine who has been through the mill of persecution blames his experiences on blind obedience to the dogma of a Perfect Book. He looks back ruefully to a time when he himself taught Scripture and "defended the Word of God" with elaborate chicanery, artful dodges, and legerdemain. He gradually grew through stages in which inner freedom, peace, and joy were his, totally harmonious with a serious appropriation of critical biblical scholarship. He longs to join hands and heart with Evangelicals of pre-critical understandings, but their fear of such new learning makes that impossible. [16]

[15] Ibid., 96.
[16] Ibid.

What a sustained sneer! Catholics can criticize Evangelicalism's approach to the Bible—we can, and we do—but what Catholic would suggest that Evangelicals' arguments defending their interpretations of the Bible are little more than "elaborate chicanery, artful dodges, and legerdemain"? Notice how Shinn's friend matured through acceptance of "critical biblical scholarship". Often "critical biblical scholarship" is nothing but a phrase meaning rejection of the Bible as inspired and in any way authoritative. When it means that, it usually also signals a palpable failing of the intellect, a kind of despair that reason can attain truth. Did Shinn's friend enjoy an "inner freedom"? Quite possibly. There is the freedom that comes with an acknowledgment of and obedience to truth, and there is the freedom (or, we should say, the simulacrum or ghost of freedom) that seems to come with abandoning truth and the search for it. When we free ourselves that way, we take comfort in looking down on people of "pre-critical understandings", even when such people include such biblically knowledgeable Catholics as Joseph Ratzinger and John Paul II.

Shinn does not seem as sure of the uniqueness of Christianity as he once may have been. He says, "The simplistic devices used in stage 3 and too often in stage 4 cause the 'true believer' to respond to world religions as if they were toys or idols. The range and vitality of Asiatic religions, for example, may be misrepresented, underestimated, and maligned." [17] True, as far as it goes, but then he goes too far.

> The world religions compete with Christians at whatever stage they are. Unfortunately, in even the most broadminded writings of stage 4 scholars, non-Christian religions are described abstractly. There is no effort to cultivate an in-depth

[17] Ibid., 97.

sensitivity to the riches and depths of understanding and
devotion the sophisticated author-teachers of those religions
represent. The in-group aggressive resistance to building
bridges of understanding and tolerance has been called "trib-
alism," a term probably most popularized by that stage 5
Baptist theologian, Harvey Cox.[18]

Cox, of course, was for years the epitome of the liberal
Protestant.

It is correct that many believing Christians do not appreciate the elements of truth to be found in non-Christian religions. This occurs because no investigation has been made,
either from lack of time or lack of interest. After all, it is
sensible for a convinced Christian—someone convinced
Christianity is true and that no important religious truth can
be found *only* outside Christianity—to put the study of Eastern religions on the back burner. The busy astronomer will
study the Copernican system and its modern offshoots because he is convinced they describe accurately the move-
ments of the planets and stars. Only if he has free time or a
particular curiosity will he learn the inner workings of the
Ptolemaic system. Granted, there are "riches and depths of
understanding" in that geocentric theory, but also error and
confusion. Is an astronomer to be called enlightened because
he declines to prefer Copernicus to Ptolemy? Call such an
astronomer what you will—but do not call him in to do the
calculations for the next shuttle launch.

"If levels suggest a ladder of ascent, Fowler has said he
would object to the picture."[19] Yes, but that may be what
needs to be said for public consumption. The fact is that
Fowler's six stages, as discussed by Shinn, are supposed to be
stages of improvement. Higher is better. After all, notes

[18] Ibid.
[19] Ibid., 98.

Shinn, Fowler "clearly favors the sophistication and scope of outlook found at stages 5 and 6. These last two stages can be linked to the highest understandings of the theme of the kingdom of God." [20] Of course, that is the view of people who are in stages five and six. Folks stuck at stages three and four might think Fowler's ladder does not go straight up, but, like a two-sided step ladder, up and down: up to stages three and four, then, on the other side, down to stages five and six. After all, a good argument can be made that the chucking of Christianity is a sign of diminishing faculties, not maturing ones.

Shinn says those "who have grown into later, more advanced . . . stages must not become condescending toward those in earlier stages" [21]—but he says this after writing the most condescending essay in *Fundamentalism Today*. Perhaps that is to be expected from a man whose final paragraph reads this way: "Fundamentalism is a pejorative term—in it is no health or healing. If more churches were centers of therapeutic growth, some traits of reactionary conservatism could be overcome and growth could be encouraged without painful or traumatic transitions." [22] The truth is that Fundamentalism is not—or should not be—a pejorative term. It can be used legitimately to describe conservative Protestants who share many doctrines with orthodox Catholics. Although we differ with Fundamentalists on many points, there is a (partial) community of belief. Let us pray we can better understand them as we try to make them understand us, and let us all pray, Catholics and Fundamentalists, that people such as Robert W. Shinn learn that discussion by sneer is not the way to go.

[20] Ibid.
[21] Ibid.
[22] Ibid.

5

Two Notions of Worship

Here is a pop quiz I give in parish seminars: "You recall that the Israelites melted down their jewelry and made a golden calf. What was wrong with making a golden calf?" Before anyone has a chance to embarrass himself publicly, I give the answer: "Absolutely nothing."

When I ask that question and give that answer, most people are stunned. "But we know making the golden calf was a sin", they say. "The Israelites were condemned for it." Actually, my listeners know no such thing. There was nothing at all wrong with fashioning a statue from jewelry. What was wrong was that the Israelites then worshiped the nonexistent god the calf represented. They committed the sin of idolatry. There never has been a sin of statue-making.

"But God expressly forbids making statues", say many Fundamentalists. They cite Exodus 20:4: "Thou shalt not make unto thee any graven image", and a statue is certainly a "graven image"—that is, an image made by human hands. When this verse is thrown at them, most Catholics are stumped for a response. If they were more familiar with Exodus, they could skip to chapter 25 and read the account of the ornamenting of the Ark of the Covenant. The Lord commanded that the Ark, which held the tablets of the Law, be topped by statues of two cherubim. The statues were to be made of gold, and the wings of the cherubim were to be held over the Ark, as though protecting it.

So here we have the Lord, in chapter 20, saying, "Don't make statues", according to Fundamentalists, and in chapter 25 the Lord says, "Make statues." The key to this apparent contradiction is the purpose behind the making of statues. In chapter 20 statues used in idol worship were condemned; in chapter 25 statues used for a proper religious purpose were praised. This brings us to statues in Catholic churches. Fundamentalists see us kneel before statues of Mary and the saints and conclude we are worshiping either the statues as such or at least the saints represented by the statues. The fact that a Catholic kneels before a statue to pray does not mean he is praying to the statue. A Fundamentalist may kneel with a Bible in his hand, but no one thinks he is praying to a book. Statues and other "graven images" are used to recall to the mind the person or thing depicted. Just as it is easier to remember one's family by looking at a photograph, so it is easier to remember the lives of the saints (and thus be edified by them) by looking at representations of the saints.

"But you pray to saints, even if you don't pray to their statues", say Fundamentalists. "That means you do worship them. At the least your prayers to saints violate 1 Timothy 2:5, which says, 'There is one mediator between God and men, the man Christ Jesus.'"

Prayers to saints, asking them to intercede with God for us, do not violate 1 Timothy 2:5. If they did, then every Christian would stand guilty of violating that verse because every Christian prays for other people. After all, what is a mediator? Merely a go-between. When we pray for others, we act as go-betweens, passing their concerns to God. Fundamentalists regularly ask one another for prayers. They are right to do this because our Lord commanded that we pray for one another. No Fundamentalist will say to another, "No, I won't pray for you. Pray to God straight!" Instead, he'll say, "I'll gladly pray for you, and please pray for me." In so praying he becomes a mediator. This does not violate 1 Timothy 2:5, which is really telling us that our prayers for one another are effectual precisely because Christ is the one mediator. Without his mediation, our prayers would be worthless.

If it is proper to ask imperfect Christians on earth to pray for us, why should it be improper to ask perfected Christians in heaven to pray for us? Death does not separate us from Christ or the Church. In fact, death brings us closer to both. Keep in mind the metaphor of the vine and the branches. Christ is the vine, and we are the branches. This is a singular vine: when a branch dies, it does not break off and fall away. It blossoms. It is perfected. Through Christ we remain in communion with other Christians on earth—and with Christians in heaven (and in purgatory). On earth we can ask for our friends' prayers by calling them on the phone, writing a letter, using sign language. The only way we can communicate with the saints is through prayer. How can they hear us? We do not know the mechanics of it, but then we do not know the mechanics of how God hears prayers either. To say he hears prayers because he is omnipotent is no answer. That still does not tell us how he does it. To claim that saints cannot hear us opens us to the claim that God cannot hear us either, and no Fundamentalist believes that.

What seems to be the real problem for Fundamentalists? Why do they get so annoyed with Catholics praying to saints? Ultimately it is because they do not have the Mass. The Mass is the highest form of worship possible—sacrifice. The Protestant Reformers did away with the Mass, so all that Fundamentalists, distant heirs of the Reformers, have to fall back on, as the highest form of worship available to them, is straight prayer. Prayer to saints can be confused with prayer to God, if prayer to God is the best one can do. The result: the worship of God may seem indistinguishable from conversation with saints.

Catholics do not have this problem. Yes, we pray to God, but we also have the Mass, which is radically unlike mere prayer and which is directed to God alone. It is easier for Catholics to keep their "honoring" compartmentalized. Despite hoary stories to the contrary, there have been almost no Catholics who have confused honoring saints with adoring God. That may be why, when Catholics see Fundamentalists kneeling with the Bible in their hands, they never think the Fundamentalists are worshiping a book. The thought just never occurs to them.

6

Note to a Seminarian

I hope you have not fallen into the trap of thinking little or nothing in Scripture is to be taken literally. In fact, nearly everything is, and the parts that are not, such as allegory, poetry, and parables, are pretty obvious. A grave injustice is done to many seminarians by making them think that Scripture is mainly metaphorical.

The problem with your Fundamentalist friend is not that he takes parts of Scripture literally but that he takes parts in isolation and takes other parts metaphorically when he should take them literally. The verses you mention, by themselves, may be susceptible to multiple interpretations, and Fundamentalists choose just one. If the verses were seen not just in immediate context but in relation to verses elsewhere in Scripture, the available interpretations would dwindle, often to only one and often to one Fundamentalists do not take.

A good example of this is the verses referring to the "brethren" of the Lord. In Scripture the word "brethren" is susceptible to two chief meanings: uterine brothers and sisters or close relatives. (A third meaning is used by Fundamentalists in their own churches: any fellow Christian is a "brother" or "sister", which is why the minister refers to "Brother Smith" and "Sister Jones", even though Smith and Jones are not related by blood.) The Fundamentalist takes these "brethren" verses in the first sense and lets it go at that. If he investigated other verses concerning Mary's perpetual virginity—or alleged lack of it—he would see that "brethren" in the narrow, uterine sense is an interpretation that will not work.

Keep in mind that, to understand the import of a verse, we need to examine, not just those around it, the immediate context, but perhaps verses far removed that do not seem to have anything to do with the issue. For instance, in pondering the relation of the "brethren of the Lord" to Mary (were they her sons and daughters or more distant relatives?), we need to be able to stand far enough back to see that while the sacred writers refer to Jesus as the "son of Mary", never once are these "brethren" referred to as the sons or daughters of Mary. This bifurcation is striking because it is abnormal. Writers tend to keep the same style throughout a work. Why refer to only one child in a family as the son of the mother? Why not refer to all of the children as the sons and daughters of the mother? Why relegate the other children to a status in which they are not ever referred to as Mary's children but only as brothers and sisters of Jesus? It is no answer to say, "Because Jesus is more important than Mary"—which is true but irrelevant to the issue. This odd usage by the sacred writers, taken by itself, does not argue toward the fact that these "brethren" are Mary's children but to the opposite. A little thought will show this, I think. These other verses do not appear in the immediate context of the "brethren of the Lord" verses, which means that if you stick only to the immediate context, even if it is extended to include the few verses before and after the verses in question, you will miss a fact that needs to be considered. Context is important, but it is not necessarily enough.

When the Jews referred to "brethren", the use of the term

was ambiguous because of the limitations of Hebrew and Aramaic (each being deficient in words for close relations, "brethren" being used instead). My point is that we cannot draw any conclusion, one way or the other, about the relation of the "brethren" to Christ if we restrict ourselves to the "brethren" verses. We must act as detectives and see if there are other verses, often far removed from these, that indicate something about Mary's relationship to these people. My argument is that there are multiple verses that are incompatible with her being their mother. While no one verse is adequate to prove the matter, all of them taken together provide a high level of confidence, approaching certainty, I think. Beyond that, Scripture is silent on the issue. There is no verse that states explicitly that the "brethren" were or were not Mary's children, and we must make do with whatever other evidence we can gather. (I abstract here, of course, from relying on authority, the Church having authority to determine this matter, even if Scripture were to say nothing about it.)

I will make one point that you neglect to allude to: you rightly note that James, Joseph, Simon, and Jude are in one verse named as Jesus' "brethren". You ignore that two of them are elsewhere named as the sons of Mary, wife of Cleophas, not of Mary, wife of Joseph. Since they cannot have had two biological mothers, they must not be children of Jesus' mother and therefore must not be Jesus' brothers-german.

I suppose if I had no preexisting belief in many Christian doctrines I would not come to them solely through a reading of Scripture—and neither would you. At least I know that many people have been unable to do so. The divinity of the Holy Spirit is a doctrine that pops to mind. It is not at all clear from Scripture that the Holy Spirit is of the Godhead.

If it were clear, we would not have seen the pneumato-machian heresies of the early centuries. One could argue, I suppose—and people did argue—that the "clear" sense of Scripture is that the Holy Spirit is God's force or influence but is not a Person—or at least not a Divine Person. It is the *sola scriptura* advocate who, historically, had a problem with the Holy Spirit verses. Those recognizing Church authority had no problem, because they knew how the verses were to be understood.

7

Blindness and the "Bible Alone" Theory

I was invited by Bill Jackson, head of Christians Evangelizing Catholics, to engage in a "written debate" with Dick Knolls, a Protestant controversialist. The subject was authority. The first installment, by Knolls, brought up a number of issues, some of them directly on point, others peripheral but interesting. In my rejoinder I concentrated on a few that seemed to demand immediate comment. Keep in mind that I was writing to a Protestant readership:

I'm grateful for this opportunity to respond to Dick Knolls' essay on *sola scriptura*. He has stated the traditional Protestant position in forceful language, and he won't object, I'm sure, if I write frankly about the Catholic position. This exchange is intended to help you obtain a rounded view of the issue of authority, and often the best way to obtain such a view is to read opposing arguments.

First, a few preliminary comments. Twice Mr. Knolls refers to the "blind followers" of the Catholic Church. He says that, "through the trickery of men" and "by craftiness in deceitful scheming", the leaders of the Catholic Church have bamboozled its members into accepting its beliefs. Since I'm a Catholic layman and not a cleric, I suppose I'm classed as one of the blind, one of the bamboozled.

I don't think this notion of Catholic laymen being tricked into being Catholics holds water, and not just because I don't like being classed with the intellectually blind. A Catholic can point to any number of clear-headed converts to his faith who are anything but blind (unless you define blindness as being the same as being a Catholic, but that's special pleading). The very fact that these people have entered the Catholic Church argues against the idea that Catholics are tricked into submission. Consider three contemporary examples.

Jean-Marie Lustiger is the cardinal archbishop of Paris. He is a convert from Judaism and is a man whose family was persecuted by the Nazis and whose conversion to Christianity cost him dearly. (His family strongly opposed his becoming a Christian.) He is a man with a sharp mind—hardly the kind who would be bamboozled.

Or consider the late Sheldon Vanauken. You might know him as the author of *A Severe Mercy*, the best-selling book about the love affair he had with his wife, who died young. Vanauken grew up a pagan (his term) but became a Protestant under the tutelage of C. S. Lewis. Late in life he converted to Catholicism. If you read his books, which are beautifully written, you will see they aren't the kinds of things that come from the pen of a man who can be led around by the nose.

As my third example, look at Thomas Howard. He was a highly respected Evangelical leader and taught at Gordon College. His book *Evangelical Is Not Enough*, written while he was a Protestant, is a plea for a more liturgical Evangelicalism. He too converted to Catholicism, seeing it as his real home. (He then lost his job at Gordon College.) Howard isn't the sort of man that can be tricked by a few rascally priests either.

I note this blindness issue because I want to impress upon you that we Catholics aren't all dolts—sure, some of us are, but some Protestants are too—and we hold our faith not because we're under the thumb of rapacious clerics but because we believe it to be true. We're people who are not ignorant about secular things; you will find many of us skilled in our occupations and in things of common knowledge. Is it likely, then, that we have become and remain Catholics for no good reason at all?

(Just as there is this "priestcraft" argument, which is given to explain why people are Catholics, there is an analogous argument, usually advanced by secularists, that people become Fundamentalists because they're ignorant, poor, and lonely. This is a caricature, as can be demonstrated easily by pointing to the many Fundamentalists who are intelligent, not poor, and not lonely.)

Often I speak before audiences that are partly or largely Protestant; sometimes the speaking is in the form of debates. When the evening begins, many of the Protestants are of the opinion that nothing can be said in favor of the Catholic faith. After all, they've never heard the Catholic side. By the time the debate concludes, they haven't become Catholics, but many of them have come to realize that Catholics have rational things to say and that there exist sensible, even if not (to them) convincing, arguments in favor of Catholicism.

Another point. Arguments deserve to be evaluated on their own merits. We don't answer an argument by saying no one but a fool would hold such a position. That isn't an answer at all. When we engage in argumentation (which, by the way, is an honorable thing to do—it needn't imply yelling at each other), we should make sure we begin at the beginning. We have to get our principles straight, and we should be clear about what we take as presuppositions.

Mr. Knolls (to return, finally, to his essay) classifies Catholicism as a cult. I won't go into why I don't think this kind of labeling is helpful. I want to direct your attention to his reasoning here. He says Catholicism "adds supplementary authorities alongside the Scripture, as do the cults. It is not *sola scriptura* for Rome but Scripture . . . and traditions with both subject to the interpretation which the teaching magisterium of Rome alone can give it." Note the syllogism: (1) A cult is a religion not based on *sola scriptura*. (2) Catholicism is not based on *sola scriptura*. (3) Thus, Catholicism is a cult. Do you see what is unexamined here? Step back from the definition of a cult, and what presupposition do you see? That Christianity is based on *sola scriptura*. But this shouldn't be a presupposition. This is something that needs to be demonstrated.

The Catholic position is that *sola scriptura* is non-scriptural. Let me put it plainly: The Bible nowhere states that the Bible alone is the sole rule of faith. The principle of *sola scriptura* is not found in Christian writings prior to the Reformation, with the exception of a very few, isolated writings that historians are unable to connect with one another and that were penned by people who did not hold what today would be called Protestant beliefs. The principle of *sola scriptura* is, in fact, an "invention", to use the word some Protestant controversialists employ to describe peculiarly Catholic beliefs.

When I make this sort of comment at a debate—when I say the Bible doesn't support *sola scriptura*—I leave the discussion open-ended. I don't give a full proof immediately. I hold off because I'm sure some Protestant listener will offer a rebuttal during the question period. He'll refer to 2 Timothy 3:16–17. The questioner will ask, "Doesn't this prove our position?"

"Not at all", I reply. Here's why. First, let's not prejudge the verse. It's been used so long as a proof of *sola scriptura* that people no longer ask, "Does it really prove this doctrine?"

Look at what's actually happening. Paul is instructing Timothy. He has just told him to hold fast to the doctrine that has been handed on to him. Then he says that everything in Scripture has been divinely inspired and that what is in Scripture has various uses. It can be used to instruct, to expose errors, to correct faults, and to educate in holy living. No Catholic denies any of this. But is the apostle saying what Mr. Knolls claims? He asks, "Can any other conclusion be validly drawn from this text except that Scripture *alone* is all that a child of God needs for instruction?" Not only is my answer "Yes", but it is that the text doesn't support *sola scriptura* in the least.

Look at the words carefully. There is no mention about Scripture being sufficient, on its own. Paul says Scripture is "profitable" for these various ends. That doesn't mean some other thing, or other things, might not be profitable also. Consider an analogy. We might say that water is profitable for bodily health—that it can help us achieve it—but that isn't the same thing as saying water is all we need to remain healthy. We need solid food and exercise too. Paul says Scripture is profitable, but he doesn't say it's the only thing that is profitable. Profitableness doesn't equal sufficiency.

That's one way to disprove *sola scriptura*. Here's another. Presume this passage did prove *sola scriptura*. If it did, it would prove too much. Let me explain. If 2 Timothy 3:16–17 proves Scripture alone is all that's needed, it must prove that Timothy had on hand all he needed. What did he have on hand? Not the Bible as we know it. The New Testament wasn't written then (and if any New Testament books were in existence when Paul instructed Timothy, they weren't yet accepted by Christians as part of the canon of the Bible). For Timothy, Scripture was what we call the Old Testament and that alone. If Paul's comment really implies *sola scriptura*, then it implies that the Old Testament alone is sufficient as a rule of faith. Does any Christian believe that? Of course not. I'm not trying to be tricky here, the way Mr. Knolls thinks Catholic priests are tricky. I'm not trying to fool anyone, and I'm not even presenting a new argument. This argument, about proving too much, is not original with me. I borrowed it from John Henry Newman—hardly a slouch in intellectual matters. Newman, who had had a born-again experience at age fifteen, was a convert from Evangelicalism to Catholicism.

Why is 2 Timothy 3:16–17 always brought up when the issue is *sola scriptura*? Force of habit, perhaps. It's always been used when one Protestant explains to another why *sola scriptura* must be true, but the Protestant to whom the explanation is made accepts *sola scriptura* anyway. He isn't inclined to test alleged proofs, to see if they really prove what they purport to prove. He doesn't take the text at arm's length and look at it from various angles.

8

Four Inadequate Reasons—and a Fifth

There are four ways to prove the Bible is true, says John MacArthur, Jr., in *Why Believe the Bible.* Unfortunately for him, not one of the reasons he gives is solid. Each, in its own way, may be convincing—that is, each of his arguments may convince someone. But bad arguments convince people all the time. The problem with bad arguments is that folks who see them today may see through them tomorrow, and then they have nothing to fall back on. Far better, surely, to be given a solid argument to begin with. But that is getting ahead of the story.

MacArthur is pastor of Grace Community Church in Panorama City, California, "where he ministers to several thousand each week". His book seems to be intended for the new Evangelical—not for the New Evangelical, a term which sometimes means an Evangelical who has lost his faith, but for the new Christian of an Evangelical bent. Strict Fundamentalists may decline to read *Why Believe the Bible* because its scriptural quotations are taken mainly from the New International Version instead of the King James Version, but, if they turn the cover, they will find little to object to. What MacArthur says can be accepted by most "conservative" Protestants.

In the second chapter MacArthur asks, "What can you say

when someone wants you to prove the Bible is true?" You can begin with the argument from personal experience. "I believe the Bible is true because it gives me the experience that it claims it will give me. For example, the Bible says that God will forgive my sins. I believe that. I accepted God's forgiveness and it happened. How do I know? I have a sense of freedom from guilt." [1]

Let's pause here. Weaknesses are popping up already. MacArthur says the truth of the Bible is evident "because it gives me the experience that it claims it will give me". If the back cover of a horror story claims the book will give you the willies and then delivers on its promise, is the story somehow true? Hardly. If a chemistry text claims to make you a better chemist than all your neighbors and then does so, does that imply everything it has taught you is correct chemistry—or have you, perhaps, been fed truth and error, but not told which is which? If a book does what it claims, does that prove it is true? Of course not.

This may be reading more into MacArthur's words than they deserve. After all, he does qualify his comment by giving an example. The Bible says his sins will be forgiven. He has "a sense of freedom from guilt", implying his sins indeed have been forgiven. Therefore the Bible is true. Sounds good, eh? The problem is that it is a lousy syllogism. The secular humanist, absorbing each nuance of *Humanist Manifesto II*, declares that he now enjoys "a sense of freedom from guilt". Is the Manifesto therefore true? If so, the Bible cannot be, and vice versa. Feeling guilt-free might mean your sins have been forgiven, or it might mean your conscience is sleeping or is malformed.

Let's continue with MacArthur's first argument. He says

[1] John MacArthur, Jr., *Why Believe the Bible* (Glendale, Calif.: G/L Publications, 1980), 19–20.

"the Bible really changes lives. Millions of people—from great heads of state to brilliant educators and scientists, from philosophers and writers to generals and historians—could all testify about how the Bible has changed their lives. As somebody has said, 'A Bible that is falling apart usually belongs to someone who isn't.' Millions of people are living proof that the Bible can put lives together and keep them that way." [2] Yes, but not only the Bible. The devout Muslim can point to the way the Koran changed his life, and the Mormon can argue that he is a better person since obeying the strictures of the Book of Mormon. Even nonbelievers can point to books that improved them. Consider the account Sheldon Vanauken gave in *A Severe Mercy* of his pagan days, when good poetry and great literature manifestly improved him. Are we to conclude, then, that Eliot and Shakespeare are inspired? Inspiring, certainly, but that is a different thing. Although reform in lives is a sign that the Bible is true, it is not itself a proof.

"A stronger argument", says MacArthur, "comes from science. Although the Bible is not a science book the descriptions referring to scientific processes are accurate." [3] He refers to the hydrological cycle: rain falls, runoff gathers into streams, streams coalesce into rivers, rivers pour into oceans, and from oceans water evaporates and forms clouds, from which rain again falls. "The hydrological cycle is a discovery of fairly modern times," claims MacArthur, "but the Bible speaks of it in Isaiah 55:10: 'As the rain and the snow come down from heaven, and do not return to it without watering the earth. . . .'" [4] MacArthur might be disappointed to discover similar comments in ancient Roman and Greek litera-

---

[2] Ibid., 20.
[3] Ibid.
[4] Ibid.

ture. After all, the observation verges on the pedestrian, and Isaiah was not expounding meteorological theories.

But MacArthur has a better scientific illustration. "Geologists speak of a state called isostasy. . . . Basically the idea behind isostasy is that equal weights are necessary to support equal weights. Land mass must be balanced equally by water mass. In order for the earth to remain stable as it spins in orbit, it must be in perfect balance. But again, the scientists haven't discovered anything that is significantly new or beyond the Bible. The prophet Isaiah also wrote that God 'measured the waters in the hollow of his hand' and that he 'weighed the mountains on the scales and the hills in a balance' (Isa. 40:12)." [5] One problem here is that MacArthur misunderstands isostasy—one may presume he is unfamiliar with the theories of Archdeacon Pratt and G. B. Airy, who in 1855 wrote about what later became known as isostasy—but you do not need to know anything about it to see that Isaiah's poetic reference to God as Creator cannot be reinterpreted to be a veiled reference to a modern geological theory.

"You can find many other examples of how the Bible matches up with discoveries of modern science", notes MacArthur. Sure, but it would be hard to point to a book of wide scope that did not have correlations with modern science. "Of course," writes MacArthur, "the precise technological language is not there, and for good reason. God wrote the Bible for men of all ages and while his word never contradicts science, it also never gets trapped into describing some precise scientific theory that becomes outdated in a few years, decades, or centuries." [6] That is true, but it is also true that "precise technological language is not there" because the Bible was not written to teach science in the first place.

[5] Ibid., 21.
[6] Ibid.

To the third proof. "A third significant area that has continued to prove the Bible's accuracy is archaeology. . . . Archaeology confirms the authority of the Bible" and "helps us see clearly that our Christian faith rests on facts (actual events) not myths or stories."[7] He is referring here mainly to things in the Old Testament, and he is quite right. Scoffers are finding themselves holding their tongues now. Once they declared the history given in the Bible to be imaginative and inaccurate, but archaeological investigations keep confirming elements of that history. So, MacArthur is right on this point, but all it means is that the Bible is being shown to contain accurate historical accounts. That does not prove the religion enshrined in the Bible is true. Edward Gibbon's *History of the Decline and Fall of the Roman Empire* may be pointed to as getting Roman history right, but are we to conclude that his unflattering comments about Christianity are to be taken as gospel truth? A book's historical accuracy is no guarantee that its religious views are right.

"Perhaps the strongest objective argument for the validity of Scripture comes from fulfilled Bible prophecy." MacArthur cites mathematician Peter W. Stoner, who "asked 600 of his students to apply the principle of probability to the biblical prophecy of the destruction of Tyre (see Ezek. 26:3–16), which claims seven definite events." These events were that Nebuchadnezzar would capture the city, that "other nations would help fulfill the prophecy", that Tyre would be leveled, that "the city would become a place where fishermen spread their nets", that "Tyre's stones and timbers would be laid in the sea", that inhabitants of other cities would worry for their own safety because of Tyre's fall, and that "the old city of Tyre would never be rebuilt."

[7] Ibid.

Using the principle of probability in a conservative manner [says MacArthur] the students estimated the chances of all seven events occurring as described at one in 400 million, yet all seven did occur. Stoner's students did a similar study on the prophecy that predicted the fall of Babylon (see Isa. 13:19). They estimated the chances of the Babylon prophecies occurring at one in 100 billion, but everything stated did come to pass. Biblical prophecy declares the events of the future with accuracy which is beyond the capability of human wisdom or anticipation. Despite astronomical odds, hundreds of biblical prophecies have come true, and they make the most objective argument for the Bible's authority.[8]

Well, if the mathematical argument is the most objective one there is, the Bible is in trouble. First of all, the argument is ill defined. How did the students come up with those numbers? If you assume an event is as likely to occur as not to occur—that is, that it has a one in two chance of occurring—then the odds that seven events will occur, as in the first example, are one in 128, not one in four hundred million. To get one in four hundred million you must assume each of the seven events, considered by itself, is very unlikely to occur. Here is another wrinkle. If Nebuchadnezzar captured Tyre and leveled it, you would expect stones and timbers to end up in the sea (Tyre was a seaport, after all) and that fishermen would use deserted pavements for spreading their nets. You would certainly conclude that neighboring people would be scared out of their wits. And so on. In other words, if a city is captured, certain other events are almost sure to happen. Some naturally go together: if A happens, B and C are implied. So instead of seven independent events, for mathematical purposes you might be talking of three or

---

[8] Ibid., 22–23.

four, and you might have to conclude that the likelihood of Nebuchadnezzar capturing Tyre was only one in one hundred million, if you want to end up with overall odds of one in four hundred million. But could it have been that unlikely that Nebuchadnezzar, the most powerful king of the region, would take Tyre?

These comments are not meant to question the fact of biblical prophecy—far from it. They are meant to show that applying mathematical formulas to the fulfillment of prophecies is almost valueless. Presumably, MacArthur would not trot out this stuff if the numbers were not so impressive. If Stoner's students had concluded the odds of the prophecies coming true had been one in ten, say, instead of one in four hundred million or one in one hundred billion, MacArthur might have realized that his argument implied a one in ten chance of the Bible being untrue, and those are uncomfortably high odds in so important a matter. No, this probability business is just too fluid for any satisfying proof to come from it.

Besides, there is a much greater problem attached to it. Even if the numbers MacArthur cites were accurate, and even if they constituted proof of inspiration, the most they would prove would be the inspiration of the particular biblical books in which the prophecies appear. They would not prove the inspiration of the Bible as a whole. Although prophecies (taken in the sense of predictions of future events) argue in favor of the faith, they do not argue in favor of the inspiration of the Bible as a whole. How can prophecies in Isaiah prove the inspiration, the truth, of the Book of Proverbs, or Ecclesiastes, or the Song of Songs (which, for example, contains no prophecies of its own)? They cannot. As soon as someone convinced by MacArthur's proofs of the truth of the Bible realizes that, he will become unconvinced.

A second-rate argument, when seen through, may be worse than no argument at all. People are likely to throw up their hands in despair.

MacArthur seems to sense this, and at the end of the chapter he falls into a kind of despair himself, asserting that there are no proofs.

> Actually there is only one argument that can prove to us that the Bible is true and authoritative for our lives: the work of the Holy Spirit in our hearts and minds. . . . While the Christian can marshal good arguments from personal experience, science, archaeology, and prophecy, he cannot finally "prove" the Bible is true and authoritative. Still, he knows the Bible is true because of his resident truth-teacher—the Holy Spirit. The Holy Spirit is the only one who can prove God's Word is true, and he does this as he works in the heart and mind of the Christian whom he indwells.[9]

In other words, the four arguments MacArthur gives are not enough. They do not prove what he inconsistently claims they prove. MacArthur's Christian must fall back on what Arnold Lunn, one of this century's foremost lay Catholic apologists, termed "fif", which stands for "funny internal feeling": The Bible is true because I feel it to be true. This is mere subjectivism, and it is no argument at all to anyone but the convinced Christian. (Even then it is a weak argument.) After all, the convinced Muslim enjoys "fif" also, but with respect to the Koran, and the atheist may feel "fiffy" when he reads Nietzsche or Feuerbach, and the glutton may conclude the only true words are found in menus, because he goes all aflutter when he enters a restaurant.

A final comment. MacArthur ends by saying the Christian "cannot finally 'prove' the Bible is true". Wrong. We can

[9] Ibid., 23, 29.

establish the Bible's truth through the application of reason. We do not have to fall back on some variant of fideism, the belief that human reason is incapable of attaining any truth apart from revelation. The truth of the Bible, which follows from its inspiration, can be established through reason. Catholics can come up with solid reasons for accepting the Bible. We do not have to rely on "fif".

PART TWO

Near the Edge

9

Looking Foolish

From Islington, Ontario, I received a letter that sheds light on the public perception of Catholics. It was from a self-described Fundamentalist who volunteered to see if he could arrange a debate between me and either Ian Paisley, theological leader of the Northern Ireland Protestants, or Bob Jones, chancellor of Bob Jones University and scion of an archetypal anti-Catholic family.

Although anxious to set up a debate, my correspondent was concerned about what might happen to me if I found myself on a platform with one of his mentors. "It does not seem fair that one like yourself, who is a layman of the Roman Catholic Church, should be made to look foolish in going into a debate with one like Paisley, who is one of the foremost authorities on Church history and the Roman Catholic religion." Now about Paisley I know little beyond what I read in the papers, and that concerns mainly Northern Irish politics, not theology. The writer might be quite right in saying I would be made to look foolish in debating Paisley—his theological knowledge might far exceed his political (Lord knows, I hope so), and, in a public talk, that could more than balance out the inherent weaknesses of his religious position. What's more, I have looked foolish when debating before, so it can happen again. I told the writer I appreciated his concern, yet I found his comment more re-vealing than he might have suspected.

He did not know me and yet was convinced I would not have a prayer against Paisley. It was not that he doubted my argumentative skills from having seen me in action; he did not base his comment on long hours spent watching me put my foot in my mouth, since he knew nothing of me beyond what I have written in various places. To him I was little more than an uppity Catholic willing to put my head on the block. I could be the best-educated, best-speaking Catholic around, but it would make no difference because his attitude had nothing to do with me as an individual, which is why I took no offense.

No matter how well trained or natively intelligent a Catho-lic might be, it is an axiom for this fellow that a Catholic cannot hold his own in a public discussion. He does not think this merely because, as a Fundamentalist, he finds the Catholic position ludicrous. There is something more. It is the belief that Catholics cannot think, precisely because they are Catholics. No matter how fine their minds before, no matter how extensive their oratorical powers, in becoming Catholics they forfeit unfettered thought and the ability to argue as they once could; they submit to a tyranny and, in doing so, give up their intellectual freedom. If they are "cradle Catholics", then they always have been hopeless. It is not simply that Catholicism is wrong, that Catholics follow mis-taken beliefs. It is worse than that. Like so many others, my correspondent sees Catholicism as a positive hindrance to thought. He thinks it shuts off the mind from anything other than what an authoritarian Church tells her members to think. No matter how smart a man might otherwise be, he does himself in, he commits intellectual suicide, by following Rome. People in other churches or no church are merely mistaken, but Catholics are mentally lost.

You might say this is just the anti-Catholic attitude common among Protestants years ago. No, it is more than that. It is not opposition to the Catholic religion in the sense one opposes some ideology because it is a mixture of error and truth, nor is it an attitude restricted to old-line Protestants. In fact, it is the (usually unacknowledged) attitude of many Americans, Fundamentalists, irreligious sceptics, and people in between. It is associated with Fundamentalists because they happen to be guileless enough to mention it. To them Catholics' inability to think is a simple fact and seems to be nothing at which Catholics should take offense, just as a paraplegic should take no offense at being told he will not win the footrace. These are just facts of life. The Islington man's comment is just the public acknowledgment of a disability—in this case, a mental disability.

His attitude arises from the notion that submission to an ecclesiastical authority stultifies the mind. In submitting, one gives up intellectual freedom for emotional security. Of course, the problem is really a failure of the imagination on the part of people who hold this man's position. They are unable to see that through submission to truth one becomes free to go after still more truth. G. K. Chesterton put it in terms of dogmas. When accused of being dogmatic, he joyfully acknowledged that the word applied, but not in the usual sense of being close-minded. Just the opposite, in fact. Our intellectual task in life, he said, is to seize upon dogmas—in whatever field—and stuff them in a bag. The more we get, the more we are able to get. In religion, if we can rely on the infallible authority of the Church, so much the better. It gives us a leg up in the most important subject of all, our final destiny. Instead of limiting what we can do, which at first glance it might seem to, this reliance on authority gives us a solid base from which to work.

Hairballs

I was debating a former priest who now heads a ministry that tries to lure Catholics into "real" Christianity. In the question period a young woman raised her hand. She looked angry and, turning to me, said, "My grandmother lives in Mexico. She is a pious Catholic. She goes to Mass every week and prays the rosary every day. Under her bed she keeps a glass jar with a hairball in it, and she worships the hairball. Why does your church promote such idolatry?" I explained to her that worshiping hairballs is no part of Catholic practice, and she seemed to accept the plea of innocence. She seemed to recognize that we should not be blamed for something we would condemn if we only knew about it. Then questions turned to real, not imagined, Catholic practices, ones that Fundamentalists find repellent. We might call these the "smells and bells" of Catholicism. These are activities that mark Catholics as Catholics, things we do that make us stand out.

On the whole, Fundamentalists dislike peculiarly Catholic customs because they think they are nonscriptural, even antiscriptural. This attitude can be overcome, but it takes patience. First, we must explain what we mean by a particular practice (many Fundamentalists do not know, say, what the sign of the cross is—they do not know the motions, and they do not know the words). Then we must explain why we do these things (because they bring to mind our Lord's redemptive work, for instance). Third, we must question Fundamentalists closely to see if they harbor some unusual misunderstanding of our practices. Many of them do. We need to impress upon them that Catholicism is a sacramental religion. Sacraments are visible signs of God's grace; they are actions that not only signify the transmittal of grace to us but really do transmit grace. They are a natural consequence of the Incarnation: God took on flesh (matter) to save us, and he left behind actions that use matter (such as water, oil, and wine) to continue to give us his saving grace. Unlike Catholicism, Fundamentalism is not a sacramental religion. It's one thing, Fundamentalists say, for God to take flesh and to use material things during his sojourn on earth. It's something else for him to set up a Church that encourages the continued use of material things. God is too great, too "wholly other", to use matter as a vehicle of grace.

Aside from the seven sacraments, Catholics have sacramentals, and in some ways sacramentals are more off-putting for Fundamentalists than are the seven sacraments themselves. Even Fundamentalists have the "ordinances" of baptism and the Lord's Supper, though they do not think these "ordinances" do what our sacraments of baptism and the Eucharist do. They have nothing like sacramentals, or so they think.

The revised Code of Canon Law explains that "sacramentals are sacred signs by which spiritual effects are signified and are obtained by the intercession of the Church" (can. 1166). They are not the ordinary means of grace established by Christ—that is, they are not sacraments as such—but they are related to sacraments. With sacramentals we consecrate our daily lives and keep thoughts of God ever in our minds.

There are seven sacraments but countless sacramentals. Any action or thing put to a sacred purpose may be considered a sacramental.

Fundamentalists use sacramentals, but they do not realize it. Consider the Protestant wedding ceremony. The bride wears white and, perhaps, a veil. She carries a bouquet. She and the groom exchange vows and rings. Each of these actions and things has a religious significance: purity in the white garments, fidelity in the vows, for instance. Each is a sign of the holiness of matrimony. Each is a sacramental (if the word is used in a wide sense). If spoken to gently, Fundamentalists can come to accept the fact that they too use sacramentals, even if they dislike the word. They are especially uncomfortable, though, when told many of these sacramentals originated in pagan religions. After all, the standard Fundamentalist charge against Catholicism is that its distinctive customs and beliefs are of pagan origin. Fundamentalists do not want to admit that they too have borrowed from paganism, but that is exactly what they have done. Their churches are offshoots of offshoots from the Catholic Church, even if they will not admit the fact. Fundamentalists believe their brand of Christianity goes straight back to New Testament times. It actually goes back only to the nineteenth century.

Let us look at a few Catholic practices that irk Fundamentalists.

Genuflecting. When they pass the Blessed Sacrament, Catholics go down on one knee to honor the Real Presence. This posture of subservience makes perfect sense since Christ is present in the tabernacle. Fundamentalists do not believe he is there, of course (they believe instead in a Real Absence), but they can be made to acknowledge the sensibleness of genuflecting through analogy. Ask them to imagine themselves at Buckingham Palace, at an audience with the Queen of England. She enters the room and walks up to a woman. Under court protocol, what is the woman supposed to do? She is supposed to curtsy as a sign of respect for the queen.

Another analogy. A soldier meets an officer on the street. What does the soldier do? He salutes. Again, a sign of respect and an acknowledgment of a superior. Who is more superior to us than God? Which Fundamentalist, transported back to first-century Palestine, would not throw himself prostrate at the sight of Jesus? If that would be proper, then why not genuflect where Jesus is sacramentally present?

Similarly, at Mass we stand when the Gospel is read, out of respect for the very words of Jesus, and we sit to listen attentively to the other scriptural readings. At the Consecration we kneel, since kneeling is the posture of adoration. What we are doing is praying with our bodies, not just with our minds, and praying that way makes sense for a creature composed of both body and soul.

Sign of the cross. Every Fundamentalist knows Catholics cross themselves when praying in church, when hiding in foxholes, and when waiting in the on-deck circle to bat. They do not, as a rule, know that Eastern Orthodox Christians also cross themselves (although they do it "backward"), so they think the sign of the cross is something that immediately distinguishes Catholics from "real" Christians. They do not know that "real" Christians began making the sign of the cross at a very early date. The theologian Tertullian, writing in 211, recorded the practice. True, the practice is not mentioned in the New Testament, but neither are peculiarly Fundamentalist practices such as the altar call, in which people march to the front of a church to announce publicly that, because of the preaching, they have just decided to "make a commitment to Christ".

The sign of the cross signifies two things at once: our redemption through the death of Jesus on the Cross, and the Trinity as the central truth of Christianity. When we make the sign, we trace the cross on ourselves, and we recite the holy invocation: "In the name of the Father, and of the Son, and of the Holy Spirit."

Incense. Not used as often in our liturgies as it once was, incense symbolizes the pleasant odor of Christian virtue and our prayers rising to God. It is the first half of the "smells and bells", and most Fundamentalists think only Catholics use incense, but incense is not peculiar to Catholics. The ancient Jews used it: incense accompanied prayers at the Temple (Lk 1:10), and one of the gifts given to the Christ Child by the Magi was frankincense (Mt 2:11). All that was before Christianity began, say Fundamentalists. Maybe so, but the book of Revelation deals with what happens *afterward*, and there we find that "the smoke of the incense rose with the prayers of the saints from the hand of the angel before God" (Rev 8:4). If there is incense in heaven, why not in churches here below?

Bells. Our church towers commonly have bells, often consisting of large sets, known as carillons, that can be rung from a keyboard. Bells have been used for centuries to call people to Mass and to sanctify certain times of the day—for instance, it once was the custom, in Catholic countries, to ring church bells at six, noon, and six so people could pause and recite the Angelus. During Mass hand bells may be rung at the Consecration, partly to focus our attention, partly to mimic the hosannas of the heavenly choirs.

Fundamentalists disapprove of bells being used in Christian worship. Why they disapprove is not clear. Some say bells are of pagan origin and thus should be forbidden, but pagans also sang hymns, and no Fundamentalist thinks Christian hymns should be forbidden. Other Fundamentalists are more straightforward: they do not like bells because bells are identified in their minds with the Catholic Church. Of course, Protestant churches often have bell towers, but that is overlooked by these Fundamentalists. For them opposition to bells is purely a matter of prejudice.

Rosary. The usual complaint about the rosary is that it violates Matthew 6:7, which reads this way in the King James Version: "But when ye pray, use not vain repetitions, as the heathen do." "See," say Fundamentalists, "you Catholics repeat prayers, and Jesus told us not to do that!" Did he really? Then how does one account for what happened in the garden of Gethsemane? There Jesus prayed the same prayer three times—that is, he repeated the prayer. Did he violate his own injunction? Was he a hypocrite? No, that is impossible, which means Fundamentalists are wrong when they claim Jesus condemned repeated prayers. Read Matthew 6:7 again. The operative word is not "repetitions". It is "vain". Jesus condemned vain prayers, such as those to nonexistent pagan gods.

The rosary is an intensely biblical prayer. It contains not only the Our Father, which Jesus himself taught us, but also the Hail Mary, which is built of verses lifted from the Bible: "Hail, full of grace, the Lord is with thee" (Lk 1:28) and "blessed art thou among women, and blessed is the fruit of thy womb" (Lk 1:42). The meditations associated with each decade—Catholics usually call them "mysteries"—are also straight out of the Bible, but most Fundamentalists do not realize this. They think Catholics rattle off Hail Marys without giving a thought to what they are doing. Not so. When we pray the rosary we meditate on incidents in salvation history, such as the Annunciation, the Nativity, the Crucifixion, the Resurrection.

Priestly vestments. Uniforms single out people engaged in particular functions. The soldier's uniform tells us his vocation, the police officer's uniform helps him be identified by someone looking for help, and the Roman collar marks the priest. Vestments—a sacred "uniform"—are used at Mass. In this the Church follows the example of the Old Testament liturgy, in which priests were dressed in special clothes (Ex 40:13–14, Lev 8:7–9), and of the New Testament, which tells us that John the Baptist "wore clothing made of camel's hair and had a leather belt around his waist" (Mt 3:4).

Holy water. Water covers most of the earth, and it is absolutely necessary for life. No wonder this marvelous liquid is used in sacraments and sacramentals. Sacred uses of water are found throughout the Old Testament: the saving of the Israelites by the parting of the Red Sea (Ex 14:15–22), the miraculous flow from the rock touched by Moses' staff (Ex 17:6–7), the crossing of the Jordan into the Promised Land (Josh 3:14–17), Ezekiel's vision of life-giving water flowing from the Temple (Ezek 47:1–12). In the New Testament we find the baptism of Jesus (Mt 3:13–17), the healing water of the pool of Bethesda (Jn 5:1–9), and the water brought forth from Jesus' side by the spear thrust (Jn 19:34). We are told by our Lord that to enter the kingdom of God we must be born of water and the Holy Spirit (Jn 3:5). With all these holy uses of water, is it any wonder the Church promotes the use of holy water? We find it at baptisms, in exorcisms, and in the stoups at the door of churches. With it we bless ourselves (there is the sign of the cross again!), not because the water itself has any special powers—it is ordinary tap water with a pinch of salt added—but because its pious use brings to mind the truths of our faith.

If we take the time, we can help Fundamentalists see that "smells and bells" flow naturally from the Incarnation, but it takes work. Many Fundamentalists are what might be termed hereditary anti-Catholics. If something is Catholic, they do not like it, period. They operate from prejudice, not from dispassionate thinking. Yet even the most prejudiced can come to appreciate the sensibleness of sacramentals if they have sacramentals explained to them by a patient Catholic.

II

Our Personal Mother

Over dinner, a U.S. Navy chaplain was recounting his experiences at what might be called an interdenominational spiritual pep rally, where the featured speaker was a well-known television preacher. During a break in the proceedings, a minister sitting next to the chaplain leaned over and asked in a serious tone, "Have you accepted Jesus as your personal Savior?"

"Yes, I have", replied the chaplain. Without missing a beat he added, "And have you accepted Mary as your personal mother?"

The minister's jaw slackened. When he recovered his composure he said, "I never thought of it like that." Most people have not. A little reflection will show that a personal relationship with Jesus should result in a personal relationship with his mother, and vice versa. If it does not, something is missing, and one's attitude toward Jesus is probably wrong.

When we look at what has happened recently, we see that as some Catholics increased their devotion to Christ (highly commendable and absolutely necessary in itself, of course), they decreased their devotion to Mary, perhaps on the theory that what is given to Mary is taken from Jesus. This might be called "the fixed-sum view of love", the idea that there is only a definite amount, so that to give some to A is to take an equal amount from B. This is a child's view of love, the view of a child who is worried that he will lose his parents' affection to the extent the new baby gets it. Parents know this is not so. In fact, the reverse is true. The new child not only gets a full measure of love, but, in some inexplicable way, there seems to be even more parental love available for the older child than before. It is a mysterious case of the parts outstripping the whole.

In the same manner, devotion to Jesus does not have to be protected by minimizing or eliminating devotion to Mary. Heightened devotion to the Mother of God results, in practice, in heightened devotion to the Son of God. When devotion to Mary falters, in the long run devotion to her Son declines. This is due to an underlying misconception about Christ. One might say the unease about giving devotion to Mary stems from a latent Nestorianism, an objection to thinking of her as *Theotókos* (literally "God-bearer", the Mother of God); this objection, in turn, comes from confusion regarding the personhood of Christ. When we look at that heresy, we see that Nestorians explained their objection to the title "God-bearer" by saying, in a roundabout way, that Christ was not one Divine Person in two natures but a moral unity of two distinct persons, one divine and one human. The logical outgrowth of *that* is reduced devotion to Jesus, because he is seen principally as man, not as God-man, and Mary is regarded as the mother of the man Jesus, not as the Mother of God.

Admittedly, talk about an old theological aberration takes us rather far afield from everyday life. One does not hear much talk on the streets about Nestorianism. Objections, within the Church, to the veneration of Mary are phrased differently: devotion to Mary is suitable only for priests (who are expected to engage in that kind of thing), elderly widows, and fuddy-duddies, or devotion to our Lady and the saints is restricted to ethnic minorities—culturally backward people who must be allowed their relics of the past—or to people whose religious instincts are not well developed. Yet there is in America a renewed interest in the Virgin and the saints, and it cuts across all levels of the Church. Much of it stems from Catholics' heightened interest in the Bible. From reading Scripture they understand our Lord to be more than just "out there", more than just an abstraction, and they seek a close and personal relationship with him. The interest in Jesus as an actual, historical person—and really God, not just a man—excites an interest in his mother—also a real, historical person—and, ultimately, in the whole notion of the communion of saints, even if that term is not used. The result is renewal of Marian devotions.

Some years ago, a few laymen started a "rosary day" in my city. It was a small affair, anachronistic to some, ignored by most, but it caught on. Three years later the organizers needed a football stadium, so large was the crowd—and what a crowd! It was not the geriatric set. To be sure, gray hairs were there, but the young were also well represented—teenagers, college students, young marrieds—and they had not been induced to attend under threat of parental displeasure. They were present because they wanted to be. It is commonly thought such gatherings occurred only before Vatican II. Has the clock been turned back? In a way it has—and all to the good. A little reaction, now and then, benefits the soul, particularly when it puts in its right place something that was unthinkingly shunted aside.

12

Churchianity

Churchianity vs. Christianity is a comic book published by a Christian commune in Geelong, Australia, a suburb of Melbourne. The publishers identify themselves as "radical, unorthodox, living-by-faith Christians". "We're a small group of people who live together. We wrote and illustrated this booklet ourselves. We believe in things like love, faith, and honesty. We spend our lives trying to make the world a better place. Other than that, we're pretty normal people." [1] Their chief bugaboo is "religion", by which they mean anything institutional, including, of course, the Catholic Church. The comic book purports to be a rephrasing of Paul's letter to the Galatians. Most panels contain cross-references to the appropriate line of that epistle. The problem is that these people, who "believe in things like love, faith, and honesty", are dishonest in their presentation.

Consider the first two panels. Paul (depicted as a bearded fellow with glasses) presents Titus to a "Churchianity" congregation. "Titus, my companion at this time hadn't even been 'baptized.' And yet no one forced him to be . . . although some tried! (2:3–4)." [2] Compare what Galatians actually says: "But even Titus, who was with me, was not

---

[1] *Churchianity vs. Christianity* (Geelong, Australia: n.p., n.d.), 26.
[2] Ibid., 3.

compelled to be circumcised, though he was a Greek."
These Australians incorrectly equate circumcision with baptism, but Paul's point in this chapter is that he "had been
entrusted with the gospel to the uncircumcised", the Gentiles, while Peter's main focus was the circumcised, the Jews
(Gal 2:7–8).

The cartoon Paul says, "The way I see it, Christ never told
us to 'baptize' with water! . . . That's a hangover from your
religious past.*"[3] Yet look at John 3:5: "Truly, truly, I say to
you, unless one is born of water and the Spirit, he cannot
enter the kingdom of God." This must mean water baptism.
Jesus does not say to be born *only* of the Spirit—he says "water
and the Spirit". Despite what some claim, he does not mean by
"water" the water of childbirth; the term is never used that
way in the New Testament. Besides, look what he does right
after this discourse: "Jesus and his disciples went into the land
of Judea; there he remained with them and baptized" (Jn
3:22). This probably means, not that Jesus himself performed
baptisms (Jn 4:1–3), but that his disciples performed them at
his direction. He must have told them to do so—a fairly clear
proof that he "told us to 'baptize' with water".

The asterisk in the last sentence quoted from the comic
book leads us to three verses: 1 Corinthians 1:17, John 1:33,
and John 4:2. These, we are to believe, demonstrate that Jesus
opposed water baptism. Here is what the verses really say:

1. "For Christ did not send me to baptize but to preach
the gospel, and not with eloquent wisdom, lest the cross of
Christ be emptied of its power" (1 Cor 1:17). Does this mean
baptism is to be opposed? Not at all. As *A New Catholic
Commentary on Holy Scripture* states, "one must hear God's

---

[3] Ibid.

[4] *A New Catholic Commentary on Holy Scripture*, ed. Reginald C. Fuller, rev.
ed. (Nashville: Nelson, 1975), 1145.

word before it can be accepted and one can be baptized."[4] Paul was writing, not against baptism, but against an *unprepared* baptism, which reduces baptism from a sacrament to a magical incantation. Jesus himself said to preach first, *then* baptize: "Go therefore and make disciples of all nations [that is, preach to them first], baptizing them in the name of the Father and of the Son and of the Holy Spirit" (Mt 28:19).

2. "I myself [John the Baptist] did not know him; but he who sent me to baptize with water said to me, 'He on whom you see the Spirit descend and remain, this is he who baptizes with the Holy Spirit'" (Jn 1:33). Again, no repudiation by Jesus of baptism. Quite the opposite, in fact. John the Baptist had been performing a nonsacramental baptism, the baptism of repentance. It was symbolic only. The baptism that Jesus instituted was a sacramental baptism because through it one received the grace of the Holy Spirit. (A sacrament is a physical sign that signifies *and* effects the transmission of grace.)

3. ". . . although Jesus himself did not baptize, but only his disciples . . ." (Jn 4:2). An apparent contradiction of John 3:22? Yes, but only apparent. Look at the full sentence: "Now when the Lord knew that the Pharisees had heard that Jesus was making and baptizing more disciples than John (although Jesus himself did not baptize, but only his disciples), he left Judea and departed again to Galilee" (Jn 4:1–3). All this says is that Jesus himself did not perform baptisms—but he certainly approved of them.

In another series of frames the Australians reject the "bondage of Churchianity", relying on Galatians 4:31—5:1,[5] but they misconstrue what Paul means. (He is talking about the Law and contrasting its salvific power with that of Christian

---

[5] *Churchianity*, 15.

faith.) The comic book refers to 1 John 4:7 ("Love is of God, and he who loves is born of God and knows God"), suggesting the Church is not necessary—love is sufficient.[6] Yet to love God fully is to love him the way he wishes, through his Church, which is his Mystical Body and which was established by him precisely as the "pillar and foundation of the truth" (1 Tim 3:15). "Don't get sucked back into churchy games", say the Australians: "To hell with your sacraments."[7] But these sacraments are Christ's and are from him. To reject them (and the ministers of them) is to reject him (Lk 10:16).

This brings us to another panel: the frustrated Paul sees a vast plot, and his Australian handlers cap the argument by saying, "Church leaders should not use titles like 'Father,' 'Pope,' 'Reverend,' etc." (Mt 23:9–10).[8] But Paul—the real Paul—uses just such a title for *himself*. "I became your father in Jesus Christ through the gospel" (1 Cor 4:15). He uses the title "Father" exactly the way we use it now—for a spiritual father. By implication he approves of the title "pope", since the word comes from the Greek and means "papa". Our biological father generates us, comforts us, feeds us, cares for us in illness. At the spiritual level our spiritual father does the same: he generates a new, spiritual life in us at baptism; he comforts us in confession; he feeds us with the Eucharist; he cares for our illness in the anointing of the sick.

What is frustrating about this comic book is not the impact it may have. What is frustrating is that it is an exemplar of a whole way of thinking. Lots of Christians chuck historic Christianity for a vague reading of the Bible. They reduce the gospel to a few pat phrases, leaving out the hard organizational sayings even when they accept most of the hard moral

---

[6] Ibid.
[7] Ibid.
[8] Ibid., 16.

sayings. Superficially, their Christianity is strong. They are zealous, and their zeal attracts others, particularly the down and out who have had their fill of "rules". But real Christianity is full Christianity; it accepts everything Christ taught, not just the convenient parts, and it accepts human nature as it really is. Our Lord told us what the Church would be like: she would be like a field of good grain mixed with tares. In other words, she would be just like the Catholic Church, containing both the elect and the reprobate (Mt 13:24–40). Many of the leaders of the Church would be grains of wheat, and the very best grains, but some would be tares. This so scandalizes some people that they do not readily accept Jesus' words. They rebel by remaking Christianity according to their own preferences. They take all the structure, all the incarnationalism, out of it, hoping to take out also all the evil, not knowing that they can take out all the evil only if they take out all the Christians.

Churchianity vs. Christianity is symptomatic of what some might call—and rightly, but only to a point—the anti-intellectual element within Evangelical Christianity. Fortunately, this element does not affect most Evangelicals, but it affects enough of them that today it affects even many Catholics. In many ways the dogmatic Fundamentalist is easier to reach than the anti-institutional Christian, the kind whose faith is best expressed through comic books.

13

Scholars Need Not Apply

From Macon, Missouri (population six thousand and just down the road from the towns of Ethel, Elmer, and Excello), comes a tract titled *Correcting the King James Bible*. It is published by a ministry called The Flaming Torch, which also publishes tracts such as *Jehoshaphatelian Fundamentalism, Scholarolatry,* and *Did Our Inspired Bible Expire?* The author is W. Bruce Musselman, Jr.

He begins by saying that the "King James Bible is being attacked daily by Roman Catholics, Jehovah's Witnesses, Mormons, Modernists, Evangelicals, and Fundamentalists." (Apparently he considers himself not just a Fundamentalist but a *real* Fundamentalist.)

> The average Christian is given a King James Bible and told it is the Word of God. From then on he hears a steady stream of criticism of it through the radio, Christian books, magazines, in church, and in Christian schools. Anyone professing to have an ounce of education and who claims to be Godly and dedicated now assumes the right to correct the Bible any time it doesn't measure up to his beliefs and standards. The King James Bible is corrected by saying 'the original says' when no one has the original. It is also corrected by saying 'the Greek says' when there are a dozen conflicting Greek texts on the market. Others say 'this is an unfortunate transla-

tion' or 'a better reading is' when they don't know enough about Greek or manuscript evidence to know what they are talking about.[1]

Then we get to the meat, which is collected into sixteen propositions. Consider a few of them.

1. "Correcting the Authorized Bible teaches infidelity. The preacher or teacher who professes to believe the Bible and then corrects it has just taught his students that the Bible has errors in it and cannot be trusted."[2] The problem with which Musselman never grapples is that the King James Version was an imperfect translation of an imperfect Greek text. It is not surprising, then, that errors occur in it, but he writes as though the English itself is somehow inspired. Indeed, he ends his tract with the statement that "correctors of the Authorized King James Bible deny God has given his people his words in the English language exactly as he wanted them given."[3] As it stands, this statement is true. Correctors do deny this because translations are not, in themselves, inspired—and Musselman seems to be referring to inspiration when he states the English words turned out "exactly as [God] wanted them given".

2. "Correcting the Authorized King James Bible reinstates the Roman Catholic Bible."[4] Now we get to his problem. Musselman complains that Catholic Bibles rely on the manuscript known as Vaticanus, so named because it reposes in the Vatican. This manuscript is faulty, says Musselman, because it was one of those composed by "the apostate Alexandrian school in the third and fourth centuries".

---

[1] W. Bruce Musselman, Jr., *Correcting the King James Bible* (Macon, Mo.: Flaming Torch, n.d.), 1.

[2] Ibid., 2.

[3] Ibid.

[4] Ibid.

Somewhat contradictorily, he says that "Catholic translations are taken from [the] corrupt Bible" that was translated by Jerome—that is, from the Vulgate, a translation not based on Vaticanus.[5] In the past most Catholic translations, it is true, were based on the Vulgate, but recent ones, such as the New Jerusalem Bible and the New American Bible, which are the Catholic translations most widely used in this country, have been based on the Greek and Hebrew, and even translations from the Vulgate, such as Msgr. Ronald Knox's, have made use of the original tongues. So, on the one hand, Musselman warns against anything based on the Vulgate. On the other, he warns against anything based on Vaticanus, which Jerome did not use.

Musselman complains that "Vaticanus leaves out most of Genesis and all of the New Testament after Hebrews 9:14."[6] Aha! A faulty manuscript and one not to be trusted—one that has been doctored! But does this follow? Why are the beginning and end of the Bible missing from Vaticanus? Was it because the copyist disbelieved in what those books taught and so dropped them from his copy? No. They are missing because the manuscript is old and falling apart, and the two ends got lost (or simply crumbled away) over the centuries.

3. "Attacking the Authorized King James Bible repudiates the Protestant Reformation."[7] That may or may not be so— probably not, since most conservative English-speaking Protestants, people who show no particular love for the Catholic faith and never have entertained an uncharitable thought about the Reformation, use English translations other than the King James or alongside the King James. Such use may constitute "attacking the Authorized King James Bible" to

[5] Ibid.
[6] Ibid., 2–3.
[7] Ibid., 3.

Musselman, but none of these people would agree to that. They would just tell you they are trying to use a more accurate translation.

4. "Correctors of the King James Bible take the same position as the Roman Catholic priest. The Catholic priest sets himself up as an authority over the Bible and encourages the people to listen to him rather than the Book. The teacher or preacher who corrects the Bible sets himself up as the authority for people to listen to, rather than the Bible, just like the priest. No wonder Bible reading is done by so few." [8] (Keep in mind that this tract is intended mainly for "Bible Christians", Fundamentalists and conservative Evangelicals who may read nothing but the Bible.)

Do priests, teachers, and preachers set themselves "over" the Bible? If he means that they interpret the Bible, the answer is yes. After all, a sermon or homily, whether Catholic or Protestant, usually deals with the meaning of the text for the day. Musselman is of the view, shared by many, that understanding the Bible takes no intellectual effort. The meaning of a verse is supposed to jump out at you, and the meaning will be perfectly clear. This sounds fine in theory. The only trouble with it is that it breaks down in practice. Brother This and Sister That will repair to their Bibles at the conclusion of the service and will discover two distinct understandings of one verse. What is the sensible thing for them to do? Why, they turn to someone more experienced and, presumably, with a better understanding of Scripture. They turn to their minister.

5. "Correctors of the Authorized King James Bible reject the wisdom of God." [9] What Musselman means is that the King James Version must be accurate because it "works".

[8] Ibid.
[9] Ibid., 4.

Missionaries have used it to convert millions, so it *must* be an entirely accurate translation. Of course, before 1611, when the King James Version appeared, there were other translations, such as the Vulgate, and these, too, resulted in the conversion of millions. Before and after 1611 there have been translations into languages other than English—for instance, Luther's German version and the German versions that preceded his—and these, too, resulted in millions of conversions. Which translation may claim the most? The King James Version can claim a large chunk of English-speaking Protestants, but not all. It can claim almost no Catholics, no Eastern Orthodox, and none of those Protestants who read no English. In other words, it cannot claim to have been the instrument of conversion for the majority of Christians.

6. "Correctors of the Authorized Bible have no final authority. They appeal to the original no one has or can have. They believe, like Einstein's theory of relativity, that everything is relative and that there is no absolute truth on this earth which a man can get his hands on." [10] First of all, Musselman has no idea what Einstein's theory means. It has nothing to do with the notion that "everything is relative" or that "there is no absolute truth." Second, why set up a particular translation as the "final authority"? One wonders how many Frenchmen, including French Protestants, believe that only the English-language King James Version is the "real" Bible.

7. "Correctors of the Authorized Bible put Christian scholarship above the God-authorized Bible. . . . While professing to believe the Bible, many schools, including Evangelical and Fundamental, have accepted Christian education as the final authority and believe it has the right to sit in

[10] Ibid., 5.

judgment on any Bible, Hebrew, Greek, or English." [11] What it comes down to—and it is not a pleasant thought—is that in Musselman's religion one must abdicate the use of the critical faculties.

Whenever we pick up a Bible, of whatever translation, we first, before doing anything else, must exercise our minds and ask ourselves: "Is this as accurate a copy of the original writings as I can get? Can I rely on this to be faithful, so far as possible, to the originals?" We do not spend much time on such questions because most of us are not capable of determining which versions are accurate and which are not. We rely on experts to produce a text for us, then we rely on the Church, ultimately, to interpret that text. In doing this we use our minds, and, however indirectly, we do make use of solid scholarship. And that is just what we *should* do.

Musselman disagrees. He is suspicious of scholarship. He has seen it go awry, as it can, and he concludes it always goes awry. He is reduced to what is either bibliolatry or the thing next to it. He suffers from an immoderate devotion to a particular translation, coupled with a rejection of all others, coupled with the idea that it is not even *possible* to have another translation as good or better. The problem with this is that readers of his tract just might buy his arguments. If they do, they set themselves up for great disappointment. If they ever stumble across good, orthodox biblical scholarship, whether Catholic or Protestant, they will be thrown for a loop. They will discover the King James Version is not specially anointed by God. Their confidence in the Bible may evaporate overnight. Having staked everything on an erroneous position, when they see that position crumble, they may see their faith crumble too.

[11] Ibid.

14

Numbers Running

Some people are infatuated with dates. I am not referring to the fruit of palms, and I do not mean taking in a movie with someone of the opposite sex. I mean numbers, as in years. Some folks like nothing better than to juggle dates and "prove" all sorts of things through apparent coincidences—which they see as more than coincidences. For instance, great import is given to the fact that Thomas Jefferson and John Adams died on July 4, 1826, the fiftieth anniversary of the Declaration of Independence. Some people see in this a divine warrant for the American political system, as though the Declaration were divinely inspired, the political equivalent of Scripture.

When a Christian is infatuated with dates, his infatuation usually has something to do with the Last Days. I came across an old booklet that argued that "the day of the Lord is near"—much nearer than many might wish. It was supposed to have come in 1992, claimed the author, Jay R. Schmarje. How did he know this? From Catholic history.

Schmarje apparently dislikes anything that smacks of ecumenism, but not because he fears some brands of ecumenism might be bad for the Catholic faith. He is no Catholic, and he does not care what happens to Catholicism as such. His interest in the Church springs from his view that Ca-

tholicism will unite with Eastern Orthodoxy and Protestantism to form a One World Church that will be in service to
the Antichrist. We are not to think of the partners in this
ecumenical enterprise as equals, says Schmarje.[1] The ringleader is Catholicism.

It all started in 962, when the German king, Otto I, was
crowned Emperor of the Holy Roman Empire by Pope John
XII. In that act a religious and spiritual leader united forces
with a political and military leader. The result was that the
papacy became subject to the temporal power. This situation,
says Schmarje, lasted until 1962. On "October 20, 1962, the
first official act of the Second Vatican Council ended what
had begun in 962", as Pope John XXIII called for discussions
on reunion with non-Catholic churches. By addressing himself to all men, not only to Catholics, the Pope began the
process of forming the One World Church. Schmarje quotes
Revelation 20:7–8: "And when the thousand years are expired, Satan shall be loosed out of his prison, and shall go out
to deceive the nations which are in the four quarters of the
earth, Gog and Magog, to gather them together to battle: the
number of whom is as the sand of the sea." Note that one
thousand years passed from Otto's coronation to John XXIII's
call for reunion discussions. What does this imply? Yes, that
the popes have been released from their subservience to the
temporal power and are (and always have been) in the service
of Satan, but it implies more than that, if we look at other
facts. It implies the end is imminent.[2]

Schmarje notes that the beginning of the first Gospel tells
us there were forty-two generations from Abraham to Christ.
Since, by his reckoning, there were 1,050 years from Abraham
to Christ, each generation was twenty-five years long. That is

---

[1] Jay R. Schmarje, "Mene, Mene" (privately printed, 1985).
[2] Ibid., 4.

fact number one.[3] Fact number two is that "Jerusalem shall be trodden down of the Gentiles, until the time of the Gentiles be fulfilled" (Lk 21:24). Jerusalem stopped being "trodden down" in 1967, with Israel's victory in the Six-Day War.[4] Now to fact number three. Luke 21:32 says that "this generation shall not pass away, till all be fulfilled." If we add twenty-five to 1967, we get 1992. So 1992 was supposed to be the year when the prophecies in the last book of the Bible were played out.[5]

Is this not amazing? Yes, and it is more than amazing. It is pitiful. First of all, the Holy Roman Empire was not started with the coronation of Otto I in 962. As every literate schoolboy knows, it began on Christmas Day, 800, when Charlemagne was crowned the first Holy Roman Emperor by Pope Leo III. One thousand years from 800 is 1800, and what happened in 1800? Nothing of consequence, apparently, or at least nothing that could be used in Schmarje's numerology. (Curiously, the Holy Roman Empire did last a millennium—and six years extra—finally being dissolved in 1806, but 1806 does not fit into Schmarje's calculations either.) All this throws out the papacy as the focus of eschatological evil and Vatican II as the event that started the countdown toward Doomsday. But let us pretend 1962 did, indeed, mark the end of papal bondage to political powers. (A better date would be 1870, when the Papal States were absorbed by Italy and Pope Pius IX became "the prisoner of the Vatican".) What about Schmarje's other claims?

A serious problem rests with the period from Abraham to Christ. We are unsure of the dates of Christ's birth and death. Most commentators say he was born between 6 B.C. and 4

[3] Ibid., 6–7.
[4] Ibid., 6.
[5] Ibid., 7.

B.C., but perhaps as early as 8 B.C. His death occurred either in A.D. 30 or A.D. 33. Which date is Schmarje using in his calculations? He does not say. If he is unsure about which date regarding Christ to choose for purposes of calculation, he should be still more unsure about choosing a date for Abraham. Many scholars say Abraham lived around 1850 B.C., but they admit they could be as much as a century off. With such imprecision at both ends of the spectrum, how does Schmarje come up with 1,050 years separating Christ from Abraham? He does not let us in on that.

For the sake of argument, let us grant Schmarje's notion that the forty-two generations mentioned in Matthew 1 turned out to average twenty-five years in length. Let us grant that the length of one generation, twenty-five years, should be tacked on to the year that Israel stopped being "trodden down", if we are to get the year of the End Times. But why choose 1967? Modern Israel was founded in 1948, after a successful war. Israel fought another war in 1956, then a third in 1967, then a fourth in 1973, all against invading Arab states. Why single out 1967? Schmarje does not say. Of course, 1948 and 1956 would not do, since adding twenty-five to them yields 1973 and 1983, years that had passed before Schmarje got around to writing his tract. Why not add twenty-five to 1973? That would give 1998, in which case we would have two possibilities: 1992, which Schmarje prefers, and 1998. Which is the right one? Schmarje comes up with further calculations—for instance, he adds thirty to 1962 because Jesus was said to be "about thirty years of age" (Lk 3:23), and the result is, again, 1992.[6] At any rate, Schmarje gets the "confirmation" he seeks. (No matter, since 1998 turned out not to be the right year either.) One could go on,

---

[6] Ibid., 9.

as he goes on, but you get his drift. Just keep in mind that this is a game anyone can play. Let us see what numerology, as conducted by Catholics, might yield.

In 535 began the Three Chapters dispute. The Three Chapters were theological writings that presented a questionable Christology. In 1535 Henry VIII declared himself head of the Church of England, and the Reformation in England was formalized. Notice that a thousand years separated these events, the first representing confusion regarding Christ, the second representing confusion regarding the Church. Henry's act sealed the success of the Reformation in Northern Europe, and, as we all know, many things have gone downhill since then. Shall we say, mimicking Schmarje, that Satan therefore was unleashed in 1535? Now to Israel. General Allenby liberated Palestine from Arab rule in 1918. That is our starting point. If we add twenty-five years to 1918, we get 1943. That year marked the turning point of World War II and the beginning of the downfall of the greatest modern enemy of the Jews, Hitler. See how it all fits together?

What do these calculations prove? That the Last Days passed us by, in 1943, and we did not even know it? That the Antichrist was born in 1943 and will make himself known any time now? That the Cubs are going to win the World Series this year? No, all they prove is that we should not pay much attention to numerology such as Schmarje's.

15

Left Behind

If you are reading this, you were not raptured. Sorry. The rapture occurred in 1988 during Rosh Hashanah, the Jewish New Year, which began at sundown on September 11 and ended at sunrise on September 13. If you had been paying attention to your local Christian radio station back then, you might have heard any number of programs devoted to the imminence of the rapture. Much of the speculation—no, not speculation: a better word is prediction—came from the fervent imagination of Edgar C. Whisenant, the author of *88 Reasons Why the Rapture Will Be in 1988.*

The book explained that Whisenant's background

> includes five degrees in technical fields, and he is an electrical engineer by trade. Edgar's name is listed on the plaque of people who helped put the first man on the moon; he is retired from NASA. His experience also includes being an instructor at the Naval Academy (Annapolis). Having the desire put in his heart by God to find the end-time solution, he set out to do it as any engineer would. His work was done methodically, and honestly, with no denominational bias. His approach for the study of Scriptures was done logically, knowing all events were sequential and had to fit in such a way as to verify and interlock with all other Bible prophecy. Edgar has never had any biblical training from any Bible

schools, just his own research, which I might add was six to fourteen hours every day for almost ten years.[1]

Reading Whisenant's short book, one suspects most of those hours were spent not reading the Bible but playing with equations. Two examples must suffice. Reason forty-four in *88 Reasons Why the Rapture Will Be in 1988* includes these proofs:

> From 2422 B.C., we have the instruction for building the Ark given by God to Noah. Thus 2422 B.C. + (9 x 490) = 1988, the year of the Church's rapture. Thus, 490 years is a period of dealing with a people (7 x 70 or 70 weeks [of 7 days]), and 9 is 3 x 3, the number of God; therefore, 9 x 490 is the end of God's dealing with the Gentile people from Noah to the end of the time of the Gentiles in 1988.
>
> From 532 B.C., the start of the Jewish punishment seven times over for not obeying God, or a punishment of 2,520 years (Lev. 26:14–39); or from 602 B.C. when Daniel told Nebuchadnezzar his dream of the idol with the head of gold, subtract the 70-year Babylonian captivity and you have 532 B.C. + (7 x 360) = 1988, the year of the Church's rapture.[2]

There are many other equations, several more just within reason forty-four. Whisenant lists "important numbers in the Bible", giving the symbolism behind 3, 7, 24, 30, 40, 49, 70, 90, 180, 280, 360, 490, 1,000, 2,520, and other numbers. Then he manipulates these until he comes up with the proper year for the rapture. More than that, he narrows it down to two days (Rosh Hashanah), and he goes on to pinpoint wars, the Second Coming, and every other event mentioned in Revelation.

You'll note the first of the two proofs given above depends

---

[1] Edgar C. Whisenant, *88 Reasons Why the Rapture Will Be in 1988* (Nashville, Tenn.: World Bible Society, 1988), 57.

[2] Ibid., 29.

on our knowing that Noah was told to build the ark in 2422 B.C. How does Whisenant know this date? Not from the Bible, which nowhere lists it. Scholars can give us the century in which Abraham lived—that is as precise as most say they can get—and Abraham lived near the beginning of recorded history, which means it becomes impossible to determine dates more than a few centuries prior to Abraham. But what if you go all the way back to Noah? We have no way of knowing when he lived—and we would have to know not just to the century but at least to the year if Whisenant's proof were to work.

Whisenant was not worried. He knew when Noah lived. An engineer, he did what any good engineer would do. He calculated it. He worked backward and determined that creation occurred in 4005 B.C. (differing with the venerable James Ussher, the Calvinist archbishop of Armagh, who calculated in the seventeenth century that creation occurred in 4004 B.C.). Whisenant determined that Jesus was born on September 29, 4 B.C. (a secret kept from all scholars until now), and that the key date for modern history was May 14, 1948, when the state of Israel was established. After that, it was child's play.

Of course, Whisenant had a little help. He relied on Meir Kahane, the rabble-rousing rabbi who, before his assassination, sat in the Knesset. From Kahane's writings Whisenant learned the importance of the number forty. He also relied on "a famous psychic [who] said that a great world leader was born at sunrise, February 5, 1962. This person may be a likely candidate for the Antichrist. It appears that Satan's events start at sunrise and God's at sunset."[3] Who was this psychic? Whisenant is coy about it, but it appears to have

[3] Ibid., 34–35.

been Jeanne Dixon, a nominal Catholic who believed in reincarnation and who survived as a reputable prognosticator despite a remarkably consistent record of inaccurate predictions.

Perhaps unsurprisingly, no one seems to have heard of Whisenant since 1989, the year he wrote a sequel explaining that in his first book he had miscalculated the date of the rapture.

16

Jeremiah's Lament

One of my favorites among the books I have never finished reading is *Romanism: A Menace to the Nation*, written by Jeremiah Crowley, a one-time Catholic priest. Published in 1912, the book has a thick purple cover with embossed gold lettering. Glued into a recess on the front is a drawing of Pope Pius X; beneath it are the lines "Our Lord God the Pope" and "King of Heaven, Earth, and Hell". The title page describes the book as "a searchlight upon the papal system"; it contains "startling charges against individuals in the hierarchy made and filed by the author and a score of prominent priests with photographic proofs and illustrations". The promotional words promise a lurid read—at least, lurid by the standards of a long lifetime ago. It was just the kind of book that would appeal to a populace suspicious of Catholicism and worried about the large influx of immigrants from Catholic portions of Europe. (My maternal grandparents had immigrated just four years prior to the publication of *Romanism*. They were the kind of people—makers of the sign of the cross—who worried "real" Americans.)

What intrigues me most about Crowley's book is the frontispiece. The photograph shows him in a formal stance: full left profile, leaning against a table, a scroll in his right hand. His wavy hair is largely gray, his coat well-tailored. Part of an elegant watch chain is visible. His facial lines are rounded, not angular, belying his age but not his weight. Halfway through the text he explains, "This book contains my photograph, and I state now that my height is six feet and three inches, and my weight is two hundred and fifty pounds." At the time of publication Crowley was fifty-one.

He was born in Ireland, ordained to the priesthood, and imprisoned by Her Majesty's Government for reasons that, on a cursory reading of his book, are unclear but probably justifiable. He left for America, settling in Chicago, where he was assigned to regular parish work, but he fell afoul of the hierarchy when he and other priests opposed the appointment of a new bishop, or so he says. He ended up excommunicated, but the excommunication may have been rescinded. I have not read enough of the book to understand even his version of the story. What is clear, though, is that by 1906 he was lecturing against the parochial school system and alleged corruption in the clergy, focusing most of his attacks on the Archdiocese of Chicago.

What kind of a man was this who stares off a page printed so long ago? What was his real story? Perhaps the photograph gives a clue. What strike me are the softness of his features and the finery of his clothes.

Crowley seems not to have been an ascetic. This is confirmed by an appeal he makes. "If I am to succeed," he says, referring to his public campaign, "I must have something more than kind wishes. I must have money! My opponents have wealth which runs into the millions. I cannot get needed publicity for the truth without money. How can I get money? The sale of a few million copies of my book would yield enough to secure a publicity of truth which will shake the

[1] Jeremiah Crowley, *Romanism: A Menace to the Nation* (Wheaton, Ill.: 1912), 215.

Catholic world as with an earthquake."[1] Ten pages later he laments, "The American clergy, high and low, exhibit an insatiable desire for money. They seek and obtain it in the sacred name of religion—for God and Holy Mother Church! Many of the means they employ to secure it are not only questionable but criminal."[2] How many readers in 1912 saw the irony here? The clergy are rapacious, but Crowley wants only the proceeds from the sale of "a few million copies" of his book.

His words remind me of an episode recounted by Archbishop Fulton Sheen. At a retreat for priests, one of the clerics complained loudly and publicly about the Church's wealth. He insisted the Church sell off artworks, cash in investments, and give the proceeds to the poor. After the session the priest came up to Sheen and repeated his remonstrances. Sheen eyed him and asked, "How much did you steal?"

"What?" said the priest, indignant.

"How much did you steal?" repeated Sheen. The priest protested. Sheen asked again, "How much did you steal?" At length the priest admitted he had been taking money from the collection basket, his rationale being that, since the Church was not a good steward of wealth, he could put the money to better use than the hierarchy could.

I wonder whether there was some of this in Crowley, a man who protesteth too much. If ever afforded the leisure, I would like to spend a few days in the archives of the Archdiocese of Chicago, seeing if a coherent story could be pieced together. What happened to Jeremiah Crowley? Does anyone still live who may have known him in his old age, if he reached old age? Was he ever reconciled with the Church, or did he end his years as a front man for anti-Catholic forces unwilling to show their own faces? I hope someday to find out.

[2] Ibid., 224–25.

PART THREE

Over the Edge

17

Why Me, Lord?

The return address was that of a prominent anti-Catholic organization. Inside the envelope were three photocopies, two tracts, and a short note to me. One photocopy was of a picture of a man in a lounge chair, baseball cap on his head, sunglasses obscuring his eyes, a drink in one hand and headphones in the other. Behind him were flames, and up on the wall was a "purgatory release chart" showing how many days had passed since his death. The caption to the picture: "15 more years or 1,010 prayers!" He seemed to be enjoying himself.

The second photocopy was of a letter to a newspaper. The writer quoted Jerry Falwell as calling the now nearly forgotten Jim and Tammy Bakker's ministry "the greatest scab and cancer on the face of Christianity in 2,000 years". The letter writer disagreed. He said, "I'm still for putting the Inquisition, the Crusades, and the performance of the Catholic Church during the Holocaust way up there over expensive dog houses, a few hundred million in tax-exempt high living, and inflicting those eyelashes on us."

The third photocopy was of an anonymous ten-stanza poem titled "A Roman Miracle". It is the story of a couple who learn The Truth about the Eucharist. The husband finally says to his wife, "To gulp such mummery and tripe, I'm not, for sure, quite able; I'll go with you and we'll renounce this Roman Catholic fable."

The tracts were no more intellectual than the photocopies. One was an excoriation of the "deception that is taken [*sic*] place at Fatima" and of the rosary. The other also was written against the rosary. It asks the reader to "look very closely at the picture of the rosary" on the first page. There are "6 steps of praying the rosary. Count the rows of black beads (small beads) and you will find there are 6 rows of beads. There are 59 beads in all plus one prayer of the Apostles' Creed on the crucifix, which comes to 60. There are 6 large beads. . . . The whole rosary consists of a complete evolution of the number 6! The real hidden mystery is 666. . . . For this is the number of the mark of the beast."

My correspondent, the head of the anti-Catholic organization, sends me such literature periodically, usually without a cover letter, perhaps on the theory I will be swayed by sheer volume if not by sheer logic. As mentioned, this time he included a note. I have changed his name and the name and city of the Catholic publisher mentioned by him. Here is the entirety of the note: "Humble yourself under the authority of Scripture. Rebellion is an outer symptom of an inward problem. When you write to Ichabod Ichabodson in Louisville, extend best wishes. I like to refer to him as 'Three-packs-a-day Mr. Ichabodson.' Thanks, Karl."

I did not think I should let this note and its accompanying literature pass without comment. I wrote the following letter to "Adam":

> Your packet of literature reminds me I didn't thank you for sending along *The Secret of Vatican Hill*. But what am I to make of the things in the latest envelope? It's hard to take them seriously. The leaflet on the rosary makes a big thing of the number six. Do you put stock in such numerology? On the

leaflet writer's own principles, you should be worried because your version of the Bible contains 66 books. The other leaflet gives the "vain repetitions" argument, which I've discussed in our magazine. It's discussed also in my book *Catholicism and Fundamentalism*, which you might want to get (and not just because you're mentioned in it).

None of the items you sent me bothered me or impressed me in the least—except your cover note. What disturbed me was your reference to "Three-packs-a-day Mr. Ichabodson." Why the name-calling, and why bring up Ichabodson's name at all? (I don't recall our ever discussing him. Your comment was entirely gratuitous.)

You advise me to read the Bible, then you say, "Rebellion is an outer symptom of an inward problem." So is bitterness, Adam. It is one thing to oppose the Catholic religion. It is something else to relish verbal swipes at people like Ichabodson. And you *do* relish them. When you stoop to that level, how can you say with a straight face that you dislike Catholicism but love Catholics? I have never come across any Catholic who refers to individual Fundamentalists the way you have referred to some Catholics. Adam, a tree is known by its fruits. You need to look at yourself objectively and see what kind of tree has produced this crop of bitterness in you.

Ten days later I received a reply:

I just returned from Kansas City to find your letter of October 29. It is apparent you are quite sensitive about name calling. Doesn't the Bible, which you "corrupt" like other Romanists do, employ name calling? Personally, I think you should be more concerned about Ichabodson's health than me referring to him as "Three-packs-a-day Ichabodson." Saying that I am bitter is a good way to hide behind gross heresy and religious blindness. You will never intimidate any of us from speaking the truth in love, which at times involves name calling. Again, dear Karl, my prayer is that you will humble yourself under the authority of God's Word. Don't be afraid to put your life on the line for the Christ of the Bible. I suggest that you desist playing the role of a psychologist, or whatever, and study your Bible more. You need a good course in systematic theology.

This letter was addressed to me in care of "Roman Catholic Lies". In the same mail, and from the same man, came another envelope, addressed to "Roman Catholic Fabrications". Inside was a copy of *1521*, a quarterly tabloid printed in Wales. It is extreme even for anti-Catholic literature. The editor of *1521* proudly reprints parts of letters sent to him: "Kindly remove my name from your mailing list . . . I can only assume that your broadsheet is the product of sadly warped minds . . . I find it appallingly bigoted. . . ." Another reader said, "I was appalled to receive your depraved and vile publication. . . . You must be a deeply damaged man if you sincerely believe that God is remotely pleased by your offensive and hurtful activities . . . this pornographic drivel. . . . This intellectually absurd and morally repugnant item." And so on.

To give you a feel for *1521*, it is enough to quote a few lines from an article about Nazi war criminals. The reader learns that "Pope Pius XII was, without a doubt, a Nazi sympathizer. . . . There can be no room for doubting that throughout the '39–45 War the Vatican wholeheartedly supported the Nazi Cause. . . . In the Roman Catholic religion, we are dealing with the most evil social, political, and religious cancer this world has seen."

You get the drift. No doubt "Adam" got it too, and I presume he sent me *1521* because he approves of its contents, just as he approves of the tracts and photocopies he forwarded. I confess I have trouble responding to the things he mailed. It is not so much that they are ill-tempered, factually wrong, and annoying—which they are—but that they are intellectually embarrassing. How can "Adam", who has been introduced to Augustine and Aquinas and, perhaps, Chesterton and Dawson and Newman, be satisfied with drivel? Here is a man who says he has a Ph.D. and who was brought up as a Catholic. He should know something about the Catholic faith, no matter how strongly he opposes it now, and something about scholarship, but one suspects he never ran across A. G. Sertillanges' *The Intellectual Life*. How could he have and yet imagine that the stuff he mails can satisfy the mind?

Maybe the problem is that I feel insulted, since I think I deserve better argumentation from him. Why can't he send a closely reasoned monograph, the kind of thing some anti-Catholics put out? Why not a letter displaying good humor and good thinking—or some humor and some thinking? Why must he try to convert me with literature that could not impress a rube?

18

The Papacy Exposed (Again)

In an article appearing in the *Signs of the Times*, a Seventh-Day Adventist publication, Robert J. Wieland explains that

the book of Revelation discloses a startling account of a diabolically clever program devised by God's ancient enemy, Satan, to counteract [God's] redemptive process. Did God intend to make the Christian church the depository of the true saving gospel? Very well, then God's enemy would design his counterfeit to assume the form of the Christian church, the better to deceive! The wolf would dress up in sheep's clothing to turn humanity away from the pure gospel. At the same time, Satan would employ the basic principles of terrorism on a global scale, exploiting deception and fear.

Wieland says the prophet Daniel pictured "the agent in this diabolical scheme as a 'little horn'—a power growing out of the ancient Roman empire, the fourth beast in Daniel's strange menagerie of kingdoms and powers. See Daniel 7:19–24." (Those verses should be reviewed now by the Catholic reader, as should verses 25 to 27 and the other scriptural passages mentioned below.)

Wieland continues:

The same power that Daniel pictures as "a little horn" growing out of the fourth terrible beast, John describes in Revelation as a beast "that derives its power from the dragon," a symbol that represents the pagan Roman Empire that ruled the world in the days of the apostles. See Revelation 13:1–2. Obviously, this "little horn" or "beast" is a religious power. It has a "blasphemous name," it receives worship, and it blasphemes God and heaven. See Revelation 13:1, 4–8. This power is out to try to wreck God's salvation program through clever counterfeiting.

Wieland does not explain how he knows that what is called a horn of a beast in Daniel is the same thing as what is called a beast in Revelation. He is on a roll, building up to an obvious conclusion, one that will be no surprise to regular readers of *Signs of the Times*. Sad to say, historically the Seventh-Day Adventist denomination and its many offshoots have been resolutely anti–Catholic, and they base much of their anti-Catholicism on what Catholics and even most other Protestants would consider an inconsequential point.

"Who is this 'little horn' or 'beast' power?" asks Wieland. "He can be no newcomer to history, for Revelation 12:6, 14; 13:5 declare that he has already ruled unopposed for 1,260 years. Numerous careful Bible students have recognized the papacy in this Bible prophecy. It fits like a hand in a glove. Notice the impressive evidence."

We will get to that evidence in a moment. First a few comments about the citations in the preceding paragraph. Let us use the King James Version. Here we have them: "And the woman fled into the wilderness, where she hath a place prepared of God, that they should feed her there a thousand two hundred and threescore days" (Rev 12:6). Notice that John is writing about a woman now, not a beast. This is "a woman clothed with the sun, and the moon under her feet, and upon her head a crown of twelve stars" (Rev 12:1). This figure, in Catholic circles, is taken to be either the Church or the Virgin Mary. Let us say the Church, since that fits best with Wieland's thesis.

Then comes the meaning of the 1,260 days. Are these regular, sidereal days? If so, they amount to three and a half years—just half of the mystical number seven. Some Protestant commentators conclude one day here really means one year, so John, they insist, must mean 1,260 years. This is Wieland's understanding. Yet the last verse he cites reads this way: "And there was given unto him a mouth speaking great things and blasphemies; and power was given unto him to continue forty and two months" (Rev 13:5). This works out to 1,260 days, not 1,260 years, but, for the sake of argument, let us accept Wieland's notion that 1,260 years are meant. Notice that he says the "little horn" or "beast" "can be no newcomer to history . . . he has already ruled unopposed for 1,260 years." Is that so? Read the verses again in light of the rest of Revelation. There is nothing that says a rule of 1,260 years (or 1,260 days) has already been completed. The rule—whatever the length of time—is yet to come. When? That is not mentioned, and there is no reason, from the Bible itself, to say the 1,260 years have been concluded, or even started, by now.

Wieland's evidence is sparse. He complains that "the papacy became the new pontifex maximus, the religious incarnation of the pagan Roman Empire. Spiritually, it absorbed the teachings of paganism while vanquishing it politically." There is a little truth here, but false implications outweigh it. The Catholic Church did take from paganism what good there was to be found in that system—and let us not deny that it had *some* good aspects, since every religion, no matter how cockeyed, has some hold on truth, else no one would adhere to it—but the Church rejected what was incorrect in paganism.

Fundamentalist Protestants consider with horror the Catholic admission that the Church borrowed from paganism, and many of them relish and even reprint a long quotation from John Henry Newman in which he admits that the Church took some of her uses, such as incense, candles, holy water, and processions, from paganism. Some of these same people are further horrified to learn that Protestantism has done the same. If paganism has infected Catholicism, it has infected every Protestant sect also. If it has infected Catholicism to a greater extent—that is, if we have "baptized" more pagan practices than have most Protestants—it is because Catholicism is a broader religion, a more encompassing religion, and one that has more room for liturgy and ceremony.

Return to Wieland's charge, that "the papacy... absorbed the teachings of paganism." This is a bit sloppy. What the papacy and Catholicism as a whole absorbed, and what Protestantism, as an offshoot of Catholicism, derivatively absorbed, were pagan practices, not "the teachings of paganism". Can Wieland name a pagan *doctrine* that is held by the Catholic Church? It is not enough to make some vague allegation about the ancients worshiping some goddess-mother and then conclude that Catholics have made Mary into the equivalent. If a Protestant controversialist argues like that, he finds himself defenseless when a non-Christian notes that the Hittites or Sumerians or Babylonians worshiped a trio of gods, and "you Christians 'baptized' that notion and came up with the Trinity, three gods in one." The Trinity is similar to a trio of gods only in that the number three exists in the consideration of each, as does divinity (though divinity of distinct sorts). Beyond that, there is no connection. Similarly with Mary and the goddess-mother. We call Mary the Mother of God, but that belief bears no relation, except the accidental, to pagan beliefs about a goddess who preceded and gave birth to the gods.

Wieland goes on. The next charge against the papacy is that it "claims an audacious authority". Quite true: it must seem audacious, if you hold that Christ conferred no continuing power on Peter and his successors. Even if you believe he did, the authority still could be styled audacious, one meaning of the word being "intrepidly daring". It *was* daring of Christ to make the earthly head of his Church a cowardly fisherman—precisely the kind of thing we would not have done had the decision been in our hands.

The next charge is that "Rome inflicted for purely religious reasons" cruelties "too horrible to contemplate" on "heretics and dissenters during the Dark Ages". Well, the Dark Ages ended before the Inquisition began, but you know what Wieland means. He admits that "Protestants as well often persecuted and tortured to death those who differed on spiritual matters", a point that would seem to argue against the papacy being the "little horn" or "beast". But he claims Catholics killed more people than did Protestants, and *that* shows the papacy is, indeed, what Revelation was referring to.

Then we get to the issue that especially bothers Seventh-Day Adventists (and other sabbatarians). Daniel says of the beast that "calendar and ordinance he shall think to set aside" (Dan 7:25). The Catholic Church, explains Wieland, abolished "the seventh-day sabbath of the fourth commandment [counting the Commandments in the Protestant fashion], substituting for it a day anciently dedicated to sun worship". This is what sets Adventists apart from other Protestants, their insistence that Saturday be reserved as the day for corporate worship. The traditional Sunday observance, observed by nearly all Christians from ancient times until 1846, when the Adventists rejected it, is something that was decreed by the Catholic Church. Everyone admits this, and the Adventists do not like it one bit. It is difficult to say to what extent their insistence on Saturday worship induced their anti-Catholicism or their anti-Catholicism induced their insistence on Saturday worship. At any rate, today's Adventists oppose the Catholic Church, in large measure because of "Sunday worship"—and, for them, that is enough to prove the papacy's real status.

Wieland's fifth point in his list of "impressive evidence" is the Immaculate Conception. His understanding of the doctrine is that Catholics think Mary *must* have been immaculately conceived; if she had not been, she could not have passed "on to Christ a nature different from that of humanity". (We do not believe he had a "nature different from that of humanity". If that were the case, he would not have had a human nature, because that is the kind of nature humans have.) If Wieland is just being sloppy here, if he means Christ could have received a sinless nature only from a sinless mother, then he finds himself trapped in an infinite regression. If Christ needed a sinless mother to obtain a sinless nature, then so did his sinless mother. And so did *her* mother, and so on, back to Eve. But Wieland says Catholics believe Mary obtained her sinless nature through a positive miracle, and thus no infinite regression was necessary. On that logic, he should have realized that Christ could have received his sinless nature directly, by a positive miracle, and not from a sinless mother— that is, he could have been possessed of a sinless human nature even if Mary had been a sinner. The Immaculate Conception was not *required* in order for him to be born. The reasons for Mary's special exemption from original sin and, consequently, actual sin had to do with fittingness rather than necessity.

Why does Wieland step into this morass? Because "the apostle John says that denying the true genetic humanity of Christ 'in the flesh' 'is the spirit of the Antichrist.' See 1 John 4:1–3." The papacy can be identified as the Antichrist because it denies Christ's "true genetic humanity", since Mary passed "on to Christ a nature different from that of humanity". The logic is strained, but that is Wieland's fifth point.

His sixth is that "most all of the world follows this religious power. Even Muslims . . . accept Sunday as the weekly day for rest, and the Pope today is the most beloved potentate on earth." (Actually, Muslims worship corporately on Friday.)

There you have it, the "impressive evidence" that demonstrates the papacy is the "little horn" and the "beast".

If one accepts Wieland's views, and his are representative of much of Adventism, certain things seem to fall into place, even if some square pegs need help fitting into round holes. He returns to the number 1,260 and says that "the papacy once suffered a 'deadly wound' when its 1,260-year political power was taken away in 1798. See Revelation 13:3. . . . In 1798 the French general Berthier took the pope a prisoner and effectively ended his temporal power. Observers thought the papacy was dead forever." True, Berthier kidnapped Pius VI, who subsequently died in exile, and the French occupied the Papal States, yet the Papal States did not disappear. They existed until 1870, when the Italian armies took control of Rome. Besides, there were many times throughout history when "observers thought the papacy was dead forever", and popes had been kidnapped before.

Look at Wieland's statement. By 1798 the papacy supposedly had exercised political power for 1,260 years. That means it first gained political power in 537 or 538, depending on whether you discount a partial year. What happened then? Absolutely nothing of consequence, except that Vigilius became pope. He had been a protégé of the Byzantine empress Theodora, who hoped to gain control of the Church through him. In that she was disappointed. Vigilius is best known for his vacillation regarding the condemnation of the Three Chapters, writings composed by men long dead by his time, but this had nothing to do with temporal power for the papacy. In fact, Vigilius was at odds with the emperor, Justinian, who kept him sequestered at Constantinople for nine years. If anything, there was a net loss of temporal power by the papacy during the reign of Vigilius.

If you want to discover the origin of the Papal States—and keep in mind that it was the Papal States the papacy supposedly lost in 1798, so it makes sense for us to look at their origin as the beginning of the 1,260 years—you will have to go more than two centuries beyond Vigilius. It was in 754 that the Papal States came into being, when Pope Stephen II entered into an agreement with Pepin, king of the Franks, at Quiercy-sur-Marne. Historian Newman Eberhardt said of the Quiercy Declaration that, "in the history of the Papal State[s], it is the closest analogy to the American July 4, 1776. . . . Henceforth the popes acted as temporal sovereigns and the Franks as their allies and protectors."[1]

Wieland himself refers to July 4, 1776. He asks, "What event triggered this sudden, amazing reversal of fortune for the papacy?" He means the events of 1798. "A seemingly insignificant revolt thousands of miles away on a new continent," he answers, "a Declaration of Independence signed on July 4, 1776, in the thirteen weak British colonies. This bold step set in motion a train of liberation struggles that has continued worldwide ever since." Like many Fundamentalists, Wieland caps his biblical interpretations with an appeal

---

[1] Newman Eberhardt, *A Summary of Church History* (St. Louis: Herder, 1961), 408.

to American history. (Religions born in America have a tendency to apotheosize the American experience. The Mormons are the best example.) It is in America, or perhaps overseas but through American might, that the victory over Satan will be won, suggests Wieland. The United States "and its Constitution have become literally the last, best hope of mankind".

Would someone please indicate where it says *that* in the Bible?

19

The Strongest Man on Earth

The Pope's Blessing is a tract written by ex-priest Joseph Zacchello. His argument, if it can be called an argument at all, is an example of the *post hoc, ergo propter hoc* fallacy: If B follows A, B must be caused by A. Zacchello attributes personal, political, and natural disasters to blessings of the popes. Since the popes are in cahoots with you-know-who, their blessings are really curses, and recipients of papal blessings are bound to end up sorry. Consider the "facts":

"1867. The pope blessed Maximilian, Emperor of Mexico. He was dethroned and shot [Maximilian, not the pope]. Then the pope blessed the Emperor's widow. She became a helpless maniac and died in exile."[1] If he has such power, why does the pope not bless today's wayward political leaders? He could keep blessing people until only the good guys are left.

"1897. The papal nuncio blessed the grand Charity Bazaar in Paris. Within five minutes it was in flames. Nearly 150 of the aristocracy perished, including the sister of the Empress of Austria."[2] Apparently Leo XIII was not only pope but a skilled arsonist.

"1924. A rich English landowner, Mr. Edwards, turned

[1] Joseph Zacchello, *The Pope's Blessing* (Havertown, Penn.: The Conversion Center, n.d.), 2.

[2] Ibid.

Roman Catholic. In 1926 he went to Rome, was blessed by the pope, and died in four days."[3] Too bad this Mr. Edwards is not further identified. We might well discover he went to Rome precisely because he knew he was dying. His imminent death may have been a foregone conclusion, and he may have wanted to view the resting place of Peter one last time. Besides, popes have blessed millions of people in Rome. Is it any wonder a few of them died while visiting the Eternal City? Lots of people die when on vacation. Yet, what if Zacchello is right? What if deaths in Rome can be attributed to papal blessings and to nothing else? Why, then, anyone seeking immortality should dash to Rome—but remember to keep out of the pope's sight!

After mentioning Mussolini, whose sad end is blamed on a papal blessing, Zacchello says, "Note also the significance of another recent prominent friendship with His Holiness. Mr. Winston Churchill called in at the Vatican, and after that he never regained his authority in Parliament. This condemnation applied equally to the late President Roosevelt, who kept a personal representative at the Vatican. For disobedience even Moses, God's chosen servant, was denied the fruits of conquest in the Promised Land. Just so has it happened to President Roosevelt, by death, and to Mr. Churchill by political oblivion."[4] Political leaders, take note.

Zacchello is not through. "General MacArthur was presented with an autographed photograph of the pope, which he considered to be one of his most treasured possessions. Soon after he was demoted as a commander-in-chief and never regained his position."[5] You do not need a blessing by the pope. A mere photo will do.

[3] Ibid.
[4] Ibid., 3.
[5] Ibid.

Queen Elizabeth is not spared. "April 13, 1951, will be remembered as Black Friday among the Protestant people of Britain. A sinister date to the superstitious, it was still more ominous for the welfare of their empire. On that day the future queen visited the pope in the Vatican, under servile and unconstitutional conditions. . . . It is very significant that after this visit to the pope, England lost the Persian oil fields, the Suez Canal, and the war against Egypt."[6] Of course, Zacchello does not inform the reader that the Suez war did not occur until 1956, five years after Elizabeth's visit. Some papal blessings, one concludes, must be slow-working.

"To be happy and prosperous," concludes the tract, "to have freedom from want and freedom from fear, a person, and also a nation, must follow King David's exhortation: 'Rid me, and deliver me from the hand of strange children, whose mouth speaketh vanity, and their right hand is a right hand of falsehood' (Ps. 144:10). The pope blesses with his right hand, a right hand of falsehood."[7]

To mollify those who are moved by complaints such as Zacchello's, should we encourage popes to bless with the *left* hand?

[6] Ibid.
[7] Ibid., 4.

20

Message from Marrs

The book's subtitle is *Peace, Promises and the Day They Take Our Money Away*. It is not about the latest plan to hack away at the deficit. It is about the millennium, and the book's title is just that, *Millennium*. But it is about more than just the millennium. It is about the New World Order, how the pope will become the head of a One World Church, and how financial moguls will take over all wealth and will attempt to wipe out America as we know it. But never fear. The author, Texe Marrs, is confident that Jesus will return just in time.

This is what Marrs writes:

> Though many Catholics will no doubt become very alarmed over the prospect, it is clearly factual that The Order desires that the Vatican be the fount and the headquarters of the New World Religion and intends that the pope of the Roman Catholic Church become the Supreme Pontiff of the whole world. The pope is to become the earth's King/Priest. He is to marshal the spiritual resources of the planet. He will also proclaim that all religions are one, that "God" has given divine authority, absolute rights, and responsibility to the World Leader. . . . It is expected that the pope will instill in peoples a keen desire to worship the goddess as the Queen of Heaven. Word will be put out to the faithful of all religions that Mary is an archetype of all the goddesses of the past,

from Isis in Egypt, Ishtar in Babylon, and Ashtoreth in ancient Israel, to Venus in Rome and Athena and Diana in Greece. "Mary" and the other goddesses will all be seen to be one and the same. It will also be promulgated that it does not matter which goddess you pray to or petition since all their spiritual energies emanate from the same source. All are to be viewed as intercessors between man and "God." The pope will also espouse the philosophy that the Great Spiritual Sun is sending to earth many rays of light and this is why there are many world religions. Each man and woman, so the claim will go, may follow the light of his or her own choosing. All men will be seen as brothers and as members of the global community. The belief that Jesus is *the* Way, *the* Truth, and *the* Life will be declared obsolete, bigoted and narrow-minded, and unloving.[1]

What is the basis for all this speculation? In the introduction Marrs explains that "there is in the world today a secretive group of powerful men who are in every sense conspirators. . . . I call these men The Lords of Money, or simply, The Order."[2] He argues that the members of The Order are out to establish a Fourth Reich. They are Hitler's heirs. Their goal is to arrogate all wealth to themselves, starting with America's wealth. These foreigners—precisely the people who have been "buying up America"—will engineer a stupendous economic collapse and will take over what little they do not already control. At that point they will be able to impose a new Final Solution, but this time on the "mongrelized race" that inhabits this country.[3]

Okay, okay. You are saying to yourself that Marrs seems to be a fruitcake, but the principles he works from infect many

---

[1] Texe Marrs, *Millennium: Peace, Promises and the Day They Take Our Money Away* (Austin, Tex.: Living Truth Publishers, 1990).

[2] Ibid.

[3] Ibid.

people, including some Catholics. I do not know Marrs and am unable to judge from personal acquaintance his sincerity, but I see no reason to rush to a presumption of good faith. His argument is so outlandish that the more natural, the more reasonable, working hypothesis is that the man is just out for a buck and that he knows where to get it: from people who lust after conspiracy theories—the more arcane or implausible, the better. The verb "lust" is used purposefully. Lust is a sin, one of the Seven Deadlies, and it does not refer only to sex. We should realize that from everyday usage, as when we read of someone who "lusts for power" or "lusts for wealth". At least as common is the lust for sensationalism or the lust (which is off-kilter desire) for being "in the know".

There have been and still are real conspiracies in the world, and some of them pan out. Just ask Lenin. Yet there are more conspiracy theories than conspiracies, and lusting after conspiracies is a spiritual (not to mention mental) failure. It is similar to lusting after signs and wonders. Just as some people search for a continual sexual high, others search for a continual spiritual high. They want to achieve a permanent state of (false) ecstasy, and they give credence to every fakir who walks down the street. We see this even among Catholics, among whom this lust tends to take the form of extreme credulity toward claims of supernatural apparitions. Authentic apparitions occur, but they are uncommon, even rare, while claims of apparitions are everywhere. Most purported apparitions are patently false, but those who lust after spiritual signs and wonders do not use their critical faculties and do not bother to make distinctions. They are not after truth so much as a high.

Those are the people, on the other side of the Catholic/ Protestant split, that Marrs appeals to, people who are never as happy as when they read about the miserable events that are just around the corner. What gives them a high is the knowledge that they will be snatched away at the last moment by their returning Lord (yes, there is presumption in that expectation) and that they are privy to facts to which others are oblivious. They are Protestant Gnostics. They revel in a secret knowledge, but the knowledge is not only untrue, it is dangerous. It is dangerous because anything that takes people away from a correct appreciation of reality is dangerous.

Pope Leo XIII said that nothing is as salutary as viewing reality as it really is. When we view reality as we wish it were, we step out of life and into a fairy tale of our own fashioning. The problem is that we then tend to treat real-world "enemies" (such as Catholics, if you are one of the Fundamentalists Marrs writes for) as we would treat scaly dragons in a fairy tale.

21

A Dangerous Morsel

On the back of the tract are two boxes. You are to check one. The first: "I choose to believe what Jesus says." The second: "I feel this tract is anti-Catholic." If you mark the second, you are told the following: "Friend, the reason we gave you this tract is because we love you and do not want to see you go to hell when you die. If you feel this tract is anti-Catholic, you had better re-examine your beliefs. Anyone who rejects what Jesus Christ says is . . . Anti-Christ. 'He that is not with me is against me' (Matt. 12:30). Please send this tract to us to let us know that after reading it you have decided to trust Jesus Christ as your Savior."

This tract is number 119 in a series distributed by the Fellowship Tract League of Lebanon, Ohio. The tract is titled *Mary's Command for Catholics*. What is her command? Turn to the account of the marriage feast at Cana. There you will read (if you have a King James Version before you, which is the version the tract uses) that "His mother saith unto the servants, whatsoever he saith unto you, do it" (Jn 2:5). "This is the only recording [*sic*] in the Bible where Mary gives a command, so most certainly all Roman Catholics should take heed to her words." [1]

---

[1] *Mary's Command for Catholics* (Lebanon, Ohio: Fellowship Tract League, n.d.), 2.

Then come juxtapositions of what Christ said with what Catholics do. "Jesus says he is the only one that can be your Savior. 'Jesus saith unto him, I am the way, the truth, and the life: no man cometh unto the Father, but by me' (John 14:6). He did not say to trust in saints, the pope, or even his mother, Mary, to save you. 'Neither is there salvation in any other: for there is none other name under heaven given among men, whereby we must be saved' (Acts 4:12)."[2] This evinces a misunderstanding of Catholic beliefs, of course. No Catholic believes he is saved by Mary or the saints, certainly not by a pope, no matter how good a man may be occupying the Roman See. Salvation is, indeed, through Christ alone. Yet prayer to the Mother of God or the saints, asking for their interventions on our behalf, does not mean we trust Jesus the less. It means, instead, that we honor and respect the salvific means he left us. He left us in the protection of an infallible Church, led by a man specially guided by the Holy Spirit; it is a Church that never has deviated from the belief that we remain one in communion with Mary and the saints and that this communion should manifest itself in communication with them.

The tract then says, "Jesus says faith in him is the only kind that can save you. 'He that believeth on the Son has everlasting life: and he that believeth not the Son shall not see life; but the wrath of God abideth on him' (John 3:36). He did not say special sacrifices or good works were needed to save you. 'But on him that worketh not, but believeth on him that justifieth the ungodly, his faith is counted for righteousness' (Rom. 4:5)."[3] This fails to take into account that Christ ordered his apostles to "do this for a commemoration of me" (Lk 22:19), "this" being a reenactment and representation of

[2] Ibid.
[3] Ibid.

his sacrifice on Calvary. Nor does the tract consider that "a man is justified by works and not by faith alone" (Jas 2:24). There is an evident tension here—some might even say a contradiction—but, whatever it is, it must be accounted for. The tract makes no attempt to do so. To understand what Christians really must believe, we cannot take into account only selected verses from the Bible.

The third point is that "Jesus says everlasting life is the only kind he gives. 'Verily, verily, I say unto you, he that heareth my word, and believeth on him that sent me, hath everlasting life, and shall not come into condemnation; but is passed from death into life' (John 5:24). He did not say it was probationary life which depended on our keeping it or we'd lose it. 'And I give unto them eternal life; and they shall never perish, neither shall any man pluck them out of my hand' (John 10:28)." [4] The third sentence in that paragraph may be poorly written, but you get the idea. Again, the writer fails to account for verses in tension with the ones he quotes. He fails to remind the reader of Paul's comment that "I buffet my own body and make it my slave; or I, who have preached to others, may myself be rejected as worthless" (1 Cor 9:27). And what about this: "Work out your own salvation in fear and trembling" (Phil 2:12)? This is not the language of someone *absolutely* certain that he is going to heaven—*morally* certain, yes, but not absolutely in the sense that there is no way he can throw salvation away and go to hell, even if he wanted to.

Next the tract argues that "Jesus says God's words are the only authority to follow. 'He that rejecteth me, and receiveth not my words, hath one that judgeth him: the word that I have spoken, the same shall judge him in the last day' (John

---

[4] Ibid., 3.

12:48). He did not say traditions or the commandments of men were his words. 'Howbeit in vain do they worship me, teaching for doctrines the commandments of men. . . . Making the word of God of none effect through your tradition, which ye have delivered: and many such like things do ye (Mark 7:7, 13)." [5]

True, Jesus "did not say traditions or the commandments of men were his words". He also did not say that "the word that I have spoken" is to be understood as meaning the Bible itself. His word, which was a spoken word, remains first of all one that continues to be spoken by a living voice, the Church. Granted, some of what he said was committed to writing, but most was not. (Demonstrate this for yourself. Get a "red letter" edition of the Bible and read aloud Christ's words. You can read them all, slowly, in a single sitting. Are we to imagine he never said more than that in three years' public ministry?) As John tells us at the opening of his Gospel, Christ himself is the Word; as he tells us at the end, not everything Christ taught or did is recorded. Christ is not the Bible, and the Bible is not Christ. The Bible records his words but is not a substitute for the Word.

What about the "traditions of men"? Again we can find verses that seem to say just the opposite of what the tract writer would like us to think the Bible says. Paul wrote to the Corinthians, "I commend you because you remember me in everything and maintain the traditions even as I have delivered them to you" (1 Cor 11:2). There is no contradiction here. On the one hand, Paul condemned erroneous human traditions; on the other, he upheld truths handed down orally and entrusted to the Church. It is these truths Catholics know by the term Tradition (with a capital T).

[5] Ibid.

This skimpy tract will not influence well-formed Catholics, but how many Catholics have even a basic understanding of their religion? How many could discuss it for more than five minutes without losing their train of thought? It is these Catholics the tract would impress—maybe imperceptibly, at a level they might not, on first reading, appreciate, but an impression would be made. A tiny doubt or confusion would be planted. From such a planting could grow a conviction to leave Catholicism for "Bible Christianity". That is why even these "throw-away" tracts should not be ignored. The problem is they work—all too well.

22

Let Me Tell You Why

One widely distributed comic book from Chick Publications is titled *Why Is Mary Crying?* It tells us that "Mary is embarrassed, because the people are bowing down to statues of her." (A photo shows Pope John Paul II kneeling before a statue of Our Lady of Fatima.) "Mary would never be a part of this because she always obeyed God's Word."[1] Just what part of the Word is meant? Why, this part: "Thou shalt not make unto thee any graven image, or any likeness of any thing that is in heaven above, or that is in the earth beneath, or that is in the water under the earth: Thou shalt not bow down thyself to them" (Ex 20:4–5). This is the commandment that Fundamentalists accuse Catholics of ignoring—and, worse than ignoring, hiding. They say the Catholic Church misnumbers the Ten Commandments and deletes this one entirely, so its people will not realize that statue worship is forbidden.

A "graven image" is a carved image or representation. The term is given here, not in limitation, but as an example, since verse 4 goes on to refer to "any likeness", which includes "graven images" but is broader, encompassing all artistic expressions. Of what things could the Israelites not have images?

---

[1] *Why Is Mary Crying?* (Chino, Calif.: Chick Publications, n.d.), 10.

First, "of any thing that is in heaven above", which includes God, the angels, and the saints. This would exclude Mary. The other things not to be depicted are those found in or under the earth, the Hebrew way of saying everything not in heaven. In other words, no images of anything at all. This interpretation, which might seem sensible if verses 4 and 5 were taken in isolation, is contradicted by the cherubim (Ex 25:18) and brazen serpent (Num 21:18) that God ordered to be fashioned. It is also contradicted by archaeological evidence, which demonstrates that Jewish synagogues were adorned with murals depicting all sorts of things found in nature.

No, it is not that the Israelites (and, derivatively, Christians) were forbidden to make images. They were forbidden to worship them. Look at the verse immediately preceding the one given in the comic book: "Thou shalt have no other gods before me" (Ex 20:3). The next two lines are not a separate commandment; they are an application of this one. In "Thou shalt not bow down thyself to them", the word "them" refers to "other gods".

This disproves the notion that the Church fooled with the numbering of the Ten Commandments. She did not, because she recognized that Exodus 20:4–5 should be read as a unit with Exodus 20:3. These verses form one commandment, the First. If catechisms usually do not quote Exodus 20:4–5, it is because they give a shortened form of the Ten Commandments. Most of the remaining commandments are abbreviated, too. Usually omitted from catechisms are Exodus 20:2b, 4, 5, 6, 7b, 9, 10, 11, 12b, and 17c. (Verses 17a and 17b are labeled the Ninth and Tenth Commandments by Catholics. Protestants put them together as the Tenth Commandment so verses 4 and 5 can be labeled the Second. The Catholic numbering is the more sensible. Read Exodus 20:1–17 and see if you do not agree.)

Return to the original charge. The real issue is bowing down to statues or other images. Bowing can be taken in two senses. The one forbidden in Exodus is a bowing that implies worship, either of the statue itself or of the person or thing represented by the statue. Do Catholics bow down before statues of the Virgin Mary? Yes, though the bowing usually takes the form of kneeling. Do they worship either Mary or statues of her? No, unless one equates worship with bowing (kneeling) itself, but you can be sure the ancients would not have done that. Most moderns would not either. In Japan people do not greet one another with handshakes. They bow. Children learn there are various types of bows: slight bows given to close friends or social inferiors, deeper bows given to employers and elders, and the deepest bow of all, reserved for the emperor. Japanese do not worship their friends, their bosses, their parents, or even the emperor, and they would laugh at you if you accused them of doing so. True, they also bow in worship at their churches, shrines, and temples, but they have no trouble distinguishing in their own minds a bow that implies worship from one that is a social courtesy.

What Protestants call the Second Commandment, part of what Catholics call the First, just does not apply to our kneeling before likenesses of the Virgin or the saints, because we do not worship the likenesses or the people represented by them. We worship only God. Why do Fundamentalists not see this? Perhaps because the honor we give to Mary and the saints, which is shown by praying to them and asking them for their intervention on our behalf, is similar to the highest honor Fundamentalists pay to God himself.

Catholics have no trouble perceiving that they worship God but venerate saints. Fundamentalists cannot see any difference, because they conclude prayer itself is worship. Granted, it can be, but it is not necessarily. It depends on the content of the prayer. Catholics pray to saints for the obvious reason—because that is the only way we can communicate with them. We cannot call them on the phone or write a letter to them. If they were still on earth, our speaking with or writing to them would not be considered worship—no one would have the gumption to make that charge—so our communication with them once they are gone should not be considered worship either. What matters is what we say in that communication, that prayer.

The second half of the comic book explains that "Satan knew Jesus would leave heaven and be born of a virgin . . . so he devised a wicked plan to confuse the people into putting their trust in a counterfeit virgin that Satan created." He found his tool in "a beautiful witch named Semiramis", who "became the Queen of Babylon and married Nimrod". We are told that "Semiramis and Nimrod came up with the idea of confessionals and celibacy for the priesthood." After Nimrod's death, Semiramis gave birth to a child "and claimed that Nimrod had been reincarnated. The child was called Tammuz. He became the sun god, Baal." Semiramis became the goddess mother and, "when the people of Babylon were scattered to various parts of the earth, they took with them the worship of the divine mother and child" under various names.[2]

"When Roman Catholicism came into existence around 300 A.D., the leaders knew if they could adopt the worship of the goddess mother into their religious system, then count-less pagans would convert to Catholicism. But who could replace the Great Mother of paganism?" Mary, of course. Today we are approaching the End Times. "Almost a billion Muslims will join [Satan's one-world church] because the

---

[2] Ibid., 15–17.

Virgin Mary was carefully placed in their holy book, the Koran. Even the 'New Agers' refer to a Mother/Father god. Satanic powers will impersonate Mary in future apparitions of the 'Virgin' worldwide . . . to bring the world under Satan's Antichrist."[3] That is why the real Mary is crying. Simple, is it not?

Or maybe not so simple. One should note that the Bible says nothing at all about Semiramis, and the references to Nimrod are few. Aside from passing mentions in Micah 5:6 and 1 Chronicles 1:10, everything we know about him is given in a few verses in Genesis 10. In that chapter there is not a word about confessionals or celibacy or anything else brought up in the comic book. The source for the Semiramis story was not the Bible but Alexander Hislop's *The Two Babylons*, a nineteenth-century anti-Catholic screed also conveniently available from Chick Publications.

---

[3] Ibid., 19, 21.

23

Deconstructing Lourdes

In a booklet called *Let's Look at Lourdes and Fatima Too!*, Muriel Webber notes that "to hundreds of thousands of Roman Catholic pilgrims who visit it each year [Lourdes] is a hallowed spot. . . . Bible-believing Protestants, however, have always held a very different opinion of Lourdes. To them it is a center where idolatry (the worship of the creature, rather than of the Creator) is encouraged, taught, and practiced. It is a place where the truth of God is obscured and well-nigh blotted out altogether by man-made traditions."[1]

Several short chapters complain that Lourdes cannot be an authentic manifestation of Christianity because the focus there is Mary, not Christ. More than that, Christ is really absent, despite the attention given by the pilgrims to processions of the Eucharist. "Even a casual reading of the Book of Acts clearly shows that Peter, Paul, and their contemporaries preached a sovereign, all-conquering Lord, to whom all authority in heaven and earth rightly belonged. *Their* God was not a Person who could be taken from place to place by men—he was omnipresent!" For all practical purposes, says Webber, Catholics keep Christ out of Lourdes.

What is kept out of this booklet is any examination of

[1] Muriel Webber, *Let's Look at Lourdes and Fatima Too!* (London: Protestant Truth Society, 1968).

cures at Lourdes. If mention of Lourdes brings to mind any thought, it is of the healing powers associated with the water. Surely this is an issue that demands attention. Webber passes over it with almost complete silence. The best she can do is to say that "sick persons allegedly find health through visiting Lourdes—but Christian Scientists and Spiritualists equally promise deliverance from bodily ills." In another place she recounts that she and her companions "looked in vain for any patient to rise from his bed or wheelchair and walk away cured". [2] That is the extent of her consideration of the miraculous cures.

Her reluctance to take them into account parallels the reluctance of those non-Christians who seem to have a dogma against the bare possibility of miracles. They may be called anti-miraculists. Their patron saint, if they have one, is Émile Zola (1840–1902), the French novelist best known for his intervention in the Dreyfus Affair. Zola took it as an article of faith that miracles are impossible. He maintained that seeing is not believing, and he had ample opportunity to see. He described the case of Marie Lemarchand, whom he saw in 1892 at Lourdes. "It was a case of lupus which had preyed upon the unhappy woman's nose and mouth. Ulceration had spread and was hourly spreading and devouring the membrane in its progress. The cartilage of the nose was almost eaten away, the mouth was drawn up all on one side by the swollen condition of the upper lip. The whole was a frightful distorted mass of matter and oozing blood." Lemarchand also was coughing and spitting up blood.

The physician who directed the medical bureau saw her immediately before and after she entered the baths at Lourdes.

[2] Ibid.

"Both her cheeks, the lower part of her nose, and her upper lip were covered with a tuberculous ulcer and secreted matter abundantly", he said. "On her return from the baths I at once followed her to the hospital. I recognized her quite well although her face was entirely changed. Instead of the horrible sore I had so lately seen, the surface was red, it is true, but dry and covered with a new skin." Other physicians examined her and acknowledged there was new skin on her face.

Zola was present. Earlier he had said, "I only want to see a cut finger dipped in the water and come out healed." The director of the medical bureau brought forth Lemarchand, looked at Zola, and said, "Behold the case of your dreams, M. Zola."

"No", said the novelist, turning away. "I do not want to look at her. She is still too ugly." He was referring to the redness of the new skin. As he left Lourdes, Zola said to the physician, "Were I to see all the sick at Lourdes cured, I would not believe in a miracle."

This is dogmatism gone mad, a complete refusal to examine evidence. It is the antithesis of the scientific attitude, but it is similar to Muriel Webber's attitude. She differs only slightly from Zola. He claimed no miracles can occur, ever. Webber claims no miracles can occur after New Testament times—and certainly not in connection with the Catholic Church. Like Zola, she is unwilling to examine the evidence—and there is evidence, lots of it, for miraculous cures at Lourdes, for the Miracle of the Sun at Fatima, and for numerous other miracles, such as the liquification of the blood of Saint Januarius. In a way, Webber's attitude is less logical than Zola's. Zola was an atheist, and he accepted no miracles. Webber's whole religion is based on a miracle—the empty tomb. Christianity depends on that unnatural occurrence known as the Resurrection. Without it, said Paul, our faith is in vain (1 Cor 15:14).

Why is Webber, why are Fundamentalists of every stripe, unwilling to look at Lourdes? It is not because they have a dogma against miracles. It is because they have a dogma against Catholicism. One suspects that, were the Virgin Mary to appear at Bob Jones University and teach that the Bible is the sole rule of faith, people like Webber might reconsider their view that miracles cannot happen in the post-apostolic age. It is the *message* of Lourdes that Fundamentalists dislike, and that message is that the Catholic Church enjoys Christ's special favor because she is the one he founded.

24

Fun Reading for Insomniacs

Looking for a good "religious" novel, one with strong char-
acterizations and a convincing plot, the kind you cannot lay
down? Well, I do not have any I can recommend, but I do
know about a real pot-boiler. It is called *The Secret of Vatican
Hill*, and it is a book with a message. The message is that the
papacy is a sham because Peter's bones are not in Rome. That
is only part of the message. That is the archaeological part.
The other part is concerned with the immediate future. The
author, Charles Allen Berry, gives us what might be called
Fundamentalist prognostication, sort of what *Lord of the World*
might have been had Robert Hugh Benson been a devotee
of Loraine Boettner or Hal Lindsey.

Berry's story begins in first-century Rome. Lucius, a fuller,
is burying his wife, Petronilla. She is laid to rest on Vatican
Hill, and the seller of the cemetery plot writes her name in
charcoal on a tile placed on the grave. There is not room for
the whole name—all he puts is "Petro"—but Lucius does not
care since he cannot read anyway. Years later, Lucius is buried
near his wife.

We skip forward nineteen centuries. Regis Hartigan, an
Augustinian priest from America, is assigned to Rome, where
he exhibits a surprisingly broad ignorance about the Vatican
and its history. He learns from a priest that there is nothing in

the tomb of the apostle—what is referred to as the tomb being the covered opening, known as the Niche, that one may see by peering over the railing into the Grotto that is in the center of the Basilica. (This happens to be true: Peter's grave is not in that Niche. It is further underground, near the tile with "Petro" on it.)

The revelation about the Niche disturbs Hartigan. His friend's "words had gone to the very jugular vein of the Church. The doctrine of the primacy of the pope stood or fell on this simple fact. If St. Peter died and was buried in Rome, then all the subsequent bishops of Rome have been his successors, and have inherited his authority, his primacy over the other apostles. But if he is not buried in the Niche, then where is the proof that he was ever in Rome? Where is the proof that the bishop of Rome has authority to create or dethrone other bishops? Where is the proof of his infallibility?" [1]

Hartigan is a worried man, and he should be worried, having such an understanding of the theory of the papacy. Assume, *per impossibile*, that Peter died elsewhere than Rome. Say his bones were discovered in Jerusalem. What would this mean with respect to the papacy? Nothing at all, because Peter would have been the bishop of Rome no matter where he ended his days. Consider the case of Pius VI, kidnapped by Napoleon's men and dying in France. Did he cease to be bishop of Rome because death came to him at an unwelcome locality? What about the popes who resided and died at Avignon? Did they retroactively cease to be popes when they died away from the Eternal City? Or maybe all these men lost the papacy as soon as they left Rome's city limits? If that were true, we have not had a pope since a few days after

---

[1] Charles Allen Berry, *The Secret of Vatican Hill* (Harbor City, Calif.: Allen & Nuri, 1987), 23.

John Paul II was elected. As soon as he left town on his first pastoral trip—poof!—it was all over.

Okay, so I am taking the principles to their absurd conclusions, but that is one way to determine if you are dealing with absurd principles. If principles lead to a ridiculous conclusion, the principles need revision, maybe even scrapping. What many critics of "Romanism" fail to do—what Berry fails to do—when they explain Catholic doctrines is to test the accuracy of their explanations by extrapolating from the principles they have outlined.

The proof of the existence of the papacy has never depended on Peter dying in Rome. It does depend on his at some point being in Rome. If Catholics can show he died there, so much the better—that establishes he was in Rome. It is not necessary, though, for us to prove where he died or where his bones are. The happy facts are, though, that we know he died in Rome—all the evidence, including scriptural, points to that—and we also know where his remains are.

Back to *The Secret of Vatican Hill*. In a flashback we see Hartmann Grisar, the famed scholar, "leaning on the marble railing of the Grotto, looking down with profound emotion at the vault below". The year is 1892. Grisar receives permission from Leo XIII to do some excavating in the Niche, and he finds—nothing! Grisar "cannot deny that the Scriptures bear overwhelming evidence that St. Peter was never in Rome for any significant period of time, neither did he establish the Church there, nor rule it." [2] Here we have what is termed "faction", a little fact mixed with a little fiction. The fact is that Grisar was in Rome and made investigations. The fiction is the sentiment attributed to him. Did Grisar

---

[2] Ibid., 26.

really think the Bible contains "overwhelming evidence" that Peter did not rule the Church in Rome? If so, why did Leo XIII even give the man the time of day?

Grisar, we are told, "returns to Austria a sad and disillusioned man. His search has proved the very fact that he had sought to disprove—that Peter is not buried under the little shrine, the so-called Tomb of Peter. Neither is anyone else. But all the while, the bones of Petronilla lie hidden under the foundation of the back wall, waiting still to be discovered." [3] End of chapter two, to a distant roll of drums.

We return to recent times. Hartigan's friend tells him that

> since Peter died a martyr's death, his body would have most certainly been tossed into the Tiber, which was the custom in those days with the bodies of executed criminals. Any attempt to rescue it, to give it a decent burial, would have been suicidal for the rescuer. The attempt would have marked him as a member of the same condemned sect. Ditto for any attempt to honor, or even to visit, his burial place. Most important, you do not build a memorial to someone without putting his name somewhere on it, or it would be self-defeating—the person and place would soon be forgotten. [4]

Hartigan does not know what to say to such arguments, but John Evangelist Walsh, in *The Bones of St. Peter*, does. Walsh explains why such arguments are groundless. [5] Your grave, for instance, might be forgotten soon whether or not your name is inscribed on the tombstone, but the location of saints' graves can be passed on by word of mouth—and would be, if Christians did not want pagan authorities to know where people like Peter were buried. To mark Peter's grave with his

[3] Ibid., 28.
[4] Ibid., 55.
[5] John Evangelist Walsh, *The Bones of St. Peter* (Garden City, N.Y.: Doubleday, 1982).

name would have been like putting a neon sign atop it: "Dig here for bones of traitor to Rome."

Hartigan is further confused when Pius XII first issues a statement that Peter's bones have been located, then admits later that the uncovered bones belonged to—a woman! ("Petronilla", of course.) "If it was Christ's plan to have a vicar on earth, in Rome," Hartigan muses, "then that pope had to be infallible—it was a dogma of the Church! Oh, maybe not infallible about insignificant things—and maybe nearly anything could be called too insignificant, if it was found later to be in error. But not this. It was much too important." [6] Poor Hartigan! He thinks popes exercise their infallibility when commenting on archaeologists' reports. Should we be surprised by this, when Hartigan's creator tells us, for example, that Pius XI was killed in 1939 by lethal injection?

The plot thickens, as we learn of general moral decay in high places, Jesuitical scheming even among non-Jesuits, and considerable confusion about the seal of the confessional. Hartigan visits the secretary of state, the pope's chief advisor. The cardinal tells him to hear his confession, then adds: "I have other things to tell you which you will regard as part of this confession, and therefore under the seal of the confessional. I give you permission to discuss these things with me or my assistants at any time, and also with Father Giordani, but with nobody else. Is that clear?"

"Yes, your Eminence, of course", replies Hartigan. "I hold the seal of the confessional in the utmost sacredness." [7] (Thank God someone does!) The cardinal goes on to tell him the Vatican's treasures are being removed to vaults in the U.S., under guise of sending them to the New York World's Fair.

[6] Berry, *Secret*, 56.
[7] Ibid., 83.

(This part of the story takes place in the early sixties.) The treasures are to be replaced with skillfully wrought fakes. All this is done because the communists in Italy are threatening to seize power and liquidate the Vatican's holdings. The first major work of art to be switched is the *Pietà*.

Then into the story comes The Woman. Every novel has one. This one is a Protestant with whom Hartigan becomes infatuated. What is a little dalliance among friends? Besides, "he never knew a priest who favored celibacy over marriage; at least, not among the ones who were normally attracted to the opposite sex."[8] Poor Hartigan, who must have known few priests and all of them of the wrong sort. He sits down and talks things over with his buddies—should they be laicized or not?—and just then Paolo gets the news that he has been named a bishop. Rats! No more chance for laicization. Priests can return to lay status, but not bishops. Paul VI, who by this time is reigning, is not *that* liberal. So Paolo takes up the unhappy duties of a successor to the apostles—his titular see is Babylon, of all places—and Hartigan is laicized and gets married. With his wife he goes into the oil business in Iraq— near Babylon, of course. Theirs is a happy marriage, but pedestrian. Consider this telephonic exchange:

> "Reggie, dear, I've been calling you for days. Where have you been?"
>
> "Honey, I've had to spend all my time at the well. So many complications."
>
> "How's it going?"
>
> "It's pretty dismal. We lost the drill down the hole and it will take weeks to fish it out. Dusty wants to quit on No. 2 and start on No. 3 . . ."
>
> "Oh, no! Does it look bad?"

[8] Ibid., 105.

"Not bad yet, dear. Dusty is betting us double or nothing on the next one, so he really believes . . . What are you laughing about?"

She laughed again. "Are you holding anything fragile? If you are, put it down. I'm coming to Baghdad!"

"You're what? For how long?"

"For good! I'm getting my discharge in a couple of weeks."

Regis was thunderstruck. "I don't believe it. How did you work that? Did you get in any trouble?"

"Yes and no. It depends on how you look at it. Reggie darling, I hope you're sitting down. We're going to have a baby!" Her voice rang with laughter like a harp stroked by an expert hand. [9]

With such scintillating dialogue to come home to, it is no wonder Hartigan spends his time concentrating on the status of the papacy. He becomes convinced that Peter never was in Rome, that when the apostle said, in his first epistle, that he wrote from Babylon, he *really* meant Babylon. Peter *did not* use the name Babylon as a code-word for Rome, as Catholic scholars always have insisted (and most Protestant ones too).

Hartigan approaches Paolo. "Paolo, you won't believe me when I tell you. I hope you're ready for this. Do you know where Peter himself said he was living in his old age—as recorded in the Bible?"

Paolo is not too swift. "Well, Rome, of course", he replies.

"No, not Rome", explains Hartigan. "Babylon! Everyone wants us to believe that when he said in his first epistle, 'The church at Babylon salutes you,' he meant 'The church at Rome.' But Paolo, I've become a believer in the accuracy of the Bible. When he wrote 'Babylon' he would have been a deceiver if he meant Rome. You don't say London if you

[9] Ibid. 164.

mean Paris, do you?"[10] Paolo had no answer to such iron logic. Why hadn't someone thought of this before?

Then it happens. One day Hartigan and his wife are driving in the desert near Babylon, looking for likely places to drill for oil. They rummage around a hillock and discover a clay tablet proving that Peter died there. The Catholic Church is thrown in a tizzy. The pope convenes a special consistory of cardinals. "Whatever they decide" about Peter's true resting place, he declares, "will be the infallible, official teaching of the Church."[11] Yet there is a danger here. "If they decide in favor of Babylon," the narrator says, "they would have to concede that the doctrine of the supremacy of the Roman pontiffs was a myth and that all their previous official acts and infallible pronouncements were totally without authority."[12] So what do the cardinals do? Right—they decide in favor of Babylon. This does not go over with all of the "four hundred million Catholics" in the world.[13] (Berry does not explain how, between 1987 and the consistory, the Church loses six hundred million members.)

While all this is going on, there is an earthquake in Rome that destroys most of the city and gives the communists an excuse to take over the Vatican. The reigning pope dies of a heart attack (and who would not?), and the cardinals elect, yes, Paolo as his successor. After all, is he not already the ordinary of the see of Babylon and the Church no longer the Roman Catholic Church but the Babylonian Catholic Church? Things go rapidly downhill from here. Paolo becomes the head of a "one-world church" with headquarters at a newly constructed Vatican in Iraq. Hartigan segues into

[10] Ibid., 151.
[11] Ibid., 208.
[12] Ibid., 216.
[13] Ibid., 218.

"real" Christianity. The two are opponents now. Paolo repeals the ban against contraception. "It was a mistake on the part of Pius XII [*sic*]", he says.[14] Other things go, and soon what is left of the Catholic Church is able to merge with Unitarians, liberal Protestants, Buddhists, and snake-oil salesmen. The name of the organization is changed to the United Nations Church.

As Paolo extends his control over the world's religions, Hartigan and his wife are forced to flee. They end up on the Caribbean island of Dominica, and from there they broadcast their message of True Christianity. Then it happens. There is a total eclipse, and darkness is everywhere. (Forget for a moment that total eclipses cover only a small part of the earth's surface.) Thunder rolls through the skies. And—*voila!*—the Hartigans and all other true Christians are missing. What happened to them? Paolo, who now is in a position to appoint the leader of the one-world government, does not much care. He does not know what the rapture is. He does not know that the elect have been whooshed to heaven, leaving the earth in control of the Whore of Babylon.

Curtain down. House lights. Applause.

[14] Ibid., 233.

PART FOUR

"It's a Wrap"

25

Analyzing an Anti-Catholic Video

Fundamentalist critics of the Catholic faith no longer restrict themselves to mimeographed tracts. Today's anti-Catholic polemicists use the latest techniques. The best example of this is *Catholicism: Crisis of Faith*, a slick, 54-minute video featuring interviews with former Catholics who claim their one-time co-religionists are not really Christian.

Produced by Lumen Productions of San Leandro, California, *Catholicism: Crisis of Faith* is packaged to look like a Catholic video. The front of the slipcase looks like a stained-glass window. The window's illustration is of priestly hands raising a host and chalice. On the back of the slipcase is a photograph of a giant statue of Mary. The words surrounding the statue are almost neutral in tone. "Follow the journey of devout Catholic clergy and laity who courageously faced a crisis of faith and emerged with a life-changing experience of Jesus Christ." This could describe a pro-Catholic video about people who rediscover their faith and become more fervent Catholics. There is no hint in the copy that the video features interviews with some of the most sharp-tongued anti-Catholics in America.

The low-decibel design of the slipcase is mirrored in advertising for the video. Spring Arbor Distributors, a major wholesaler of mainly Evangelical books and tapes, carried in its catalogues an ad that called *Catholicism: Crisis of Faith* "an ideal training resource for churches, Bible schools, seminaries, and mission agencies. Learn of the doctrines and practices of the Roman Catholic Church and how they compare with Scripture." No screeds mar this advertising; there is no hint of anti-Catholicism.

Spring Arbor's promotional blurb from Hal Lindsey, author of the best-selling *Late Great Planet Earth*, said the video "presents a startling investigation of the world's largest religious denomination. . . . Must see for anyone seeking to understand the times in which we live."

John MacArthur, Jr., pastor, author, and radio personality, said in his blurb, "I appreciate very much the direct, clear, biblical treatment of Catholicism. . . . For anyone who wants a clear understanding of how Catholic theology differs from the Bible, this is a helpful tool."

Even Dave Hunt, author of sensationalistic anti-Catholic books, was muted: "Everyone needs to see this video, which cannot be commended too highly. And I especially recommend the accompanying annotated transcript", available from Lumen Productions. (I have debated Hunt several times on radio and television. Usually he tries to take the last word in the exchange, and he prefers the last word to be comprised of passages from Alphonsus Liguori, who, when writing about Mary, used exceptionally flowery language in his praises of her. When taken out of context and without an understanding of his milieu and his century's literary forms, Liguori's remarks seem to exceed the bounds of propriety. The last time Hunt tried to use this technique I butted in and used up the show's remaining seconds with my own comments. In apologetics you cannot afford to be a wallflower.)

Christianity Today, the Evangelical monthly founded by Billy Graham, ran full-page ads for the video. Generally considered to be the flagship publication of Evangelicalism, *Christianity Today* nowadays takes, if not an irenic stand toward Catholicism, at least a polite stand, though on occasion it publishes columns that fall into traditional anti-Catholic rhetoric. In the ad in *Christianity Today* MacArthur was quoted again, saying, "This is so needed today when ecumenical efforts have done everything to blur the lines and to endorse the heresy as if it were truth." (Okay, so not everyone is muted.) The ad copy explained that "*Catholicism: Crisis of Faith* is also for Catholics. Produced by former Catholics, this film approaches the subject with care and sensitivity. It gives former priests and nuns the opportunity to speak with compassion to the sincere people they had sought to serve with their lives. Here is an effective evangelization tool you will be pleased to share with seeking family and friends."

Lumen Productions was begun by James G. McCarthy, a former Catholic who left the Church in 1977. His attitude about "Romanism" is unmistakable: "I could not remain in the Catholic Church and claim to be trusting Christ fully for my salvation. Every Mass, sacrament, penance, and offering is an insult to the finished work of Christ." McCarthy refuses to reveal how many copies of *Catholicism: Crisis of Faith* have been sold, but, if the ubiquity of the ads is any indication, this video has become one of Fundamentalism's most effective attacks on the Catholic Church. It reiterates the Fundamentalist argument that, as McCarthy puts it, "Roman Catholicism has added to the Christian faith and to the gospel itself from the traditions of men."

Aside from Lumen Productions, McCarthy runs a ministry called Good News for Catholics. The ministry came first, the video production operation later. One issue of the ministry's newsletter carried a letter from an unnamed Dominican nun. She charged that in the video "priests in good standing with the Catholic Church were quoted out of context and made to appear ridiculous." McCarthy answered her, "I assure you that no interview was taken out of context", but that is not what one of the priests interviewed said.

Father Richard Chilson, a Paulist, has written several books, among them *Catholic Christianity* and *An Introduction to the Faith of Catholics*. "McCarthy approached me saying that they were doing a video to help Christians understand the Catholic Church. He was all sweetness and ecumenism. I spend a lot of my ministry fighting Fundamentalists, and I must admit to having been duped by this one. I figured they were Evangelical Christians rather than Fundamentalists and so agreed to cooperate in the interview. There was no preparation for the interview other than that I knew they wanted me to speak about the current state of Catholicism." The interview lasted an hour and a half and covered a wide range of subjects, including "the crisis in the Church today, the shortage of priests, and dissent". After the interview Chilson asked to see the finished video. He never was sent a copy and never had a chance to review his edited interview. No theatrical release was given to him to sign, but some months later he received a check for $125. (McCarthy says all interviewees signed releases.) Chilson forgot about the video entirely until, while at a convention, "some women approached me and asked if I were the priest in this video. They told me that it was pretty biased and suggested I could go down to Hayward [California] where they would show it to me."

Much of the Chilson interview concerned the Mass as a sacrifice. "The first extended quote they have from me in the video is part of that explanation, but it is not easy to give the Catholic understanding of Eucharistic sacrifice in a sound bite. That discussion went on for at least fifteen minutes, and McCarthy kept coming back to the idea of sacrifice."

Then comes a bit of slick editing. The voice-over narrator says, "Other Christian denominations celebrate that the sacrifice is finished. We asked Father Chilson why the Catholic Church chooses to focus on it continuing. Why not leave it finished?" The visuals show Chilson leaning back in his chair and passing his hand across his head, as though searching for an answer. He looks weary and replies, "I don't know if I can answer that. I am sorry. I know that's—that's a real issue between Protestants and Catholics, but I don't know if I can answer it in any better way than I've already kind of stumbled on." The video cuts to Frank Eberhardt, once a Catholic seminarian and now a Fundamentalist proselytizer of Catholics. He says, "The Catholic priest cannot really explain how that the finished work of Christ on the cross is continued today in the Mass."

"They of course made it look like I had nothing to say," says Chilson, "whereas I had been trying to explain the issue for a good quarter hour. I would stand by what I said in the first shot, although, taken out of context, it does not stand well on its own. The second shot is dirty pool. Indeed, I was suspicious that my response there may not even have been to that exact question. But even if it was, this was not lack of an answer on my part but frustration and exhaustion at going over the same ground again and again."

Chilson notes wryly that in the interview as much time was spent on salvation as on the Eucharist, but "none of that was used because I gave them the gospel answer of salvation through Jesus Christ. Certainly biased sampling was at work. If you fit their stereotype of a Catholic, you were on screen. If you presented the gospel, you were ignored. I have to deal with this continually from Fundamentalists. The response is invariably that you are an exceptional Catholic" if you present the Catholic understanding of salvation as it really is—not as

Fundamentalists think Catholics think it is. "You become an exception that proves the rule."

As though to prove Chilson's charge of selective editing, former priest Bart Brewer says in the video, "The Catholic gospel, the Roman Catholic gospel, is absolutely a gospel of works." But in the transcript we find a footnote to Brewer's remark: "The Council of Trent dogmatically stated the Catholic position as follows: 'If anyone says that the justice received is not preserved and also not increased before God through good works, but that those works are merely the fruits and signs of justification obtained, but not the cause of its increase, let him be anathema (cursed).'" One begins to wonder whether this line from Trent has been read slowly by the author of the transcript's footnotes. It is not referring to how we initially obtain justification—the Council says we obtain it by grace through faith, not through good works— but to how our sanctification (the word commonly used by Protestants) is increased by our good works after we are justi- fied and how that initial justification is preserved by our good works (because by doing good works we stay away from evil works, sins, through which we can forfeit justification). Even Fundamentalists talk about a process of sanctification that comes after justification, yet the passage from Trent has been misconstrued to mean something that the Catholic Church does not teach but that Fundamentalists think she teaches. (By the way, contrary to what the transcript says, "let him be anathema" is not properly translated as "let him be cursed" [to hell]. In ecclesiastical documents "let him be anathema" means "let him be excommunicated.")

Chilson, whose doctoral work has been in Mahayana Bud- dhism, with a specialty in Tibetan Buddhism, says he se- lected this area of study because Buddhism "seemed to be as contrary to Christianity as it was possible to be". The video quotes him as saying that, although Buddhists do not believe in God or the soul, behind their myths is a reality that corresponds to the reality addressed by Christianity. In this Chilson, properly understood, is quite correct. It is only to be expected that, since all people face the same reality around them, even those without access to authentic revelation are able to grasp certain elements of that reality accurately— while misconstruing others, of course. Even Buddhists get some things right. The narrator's comments before and after Chilson's brief remarks on Buddhism lead the viewer to believe that Chilson in particular and the Catholic Church in general are working toward some vague amalgamation of Catholicism and Buddhism, something not actually implied in Chilson's remarks. "As to what I said on Buddhism and non-Christian religions, I would stand by it, but again it is taken out of context. This interview was not done as sound bites, but as a long, leisurely conversation. If I had been doing sound bites, I would have needed a lot more time for thought than simply what came to mind as an immediate response to the question."

Chilson's experience with McCarthy and the interview has not heightened his desire to engage in discussions with Fundamentalists. "One of the Paulists watching [the video] with me said at the end that perhaps we should not be engaged in ecumenical dialogue [with Fundamentalists], which is one of the three major Paulist ministries." The sentiment is understandable, even though neither Chilson nor his fellow Paulist probably feels quite that way now that their anger has cooled.

If Chilson was the victim of slick editing, so were anonymous Catholics interviewed outside Saint Patrick's Cathedral in New York City. Neither the video nor the transcript indicates the total number of Catholics who were interviewed.

Perhaps only the ones giving the "best" answers ended up featured in *Catholicism: Crisis of Faith*. All the viewer sees is the narrator asking nine lay Catholics—presumably representative of all lay Catholics—how they think they can get to heaven. The responses are not encouraging.

"Well, you know, by being a good Catholic and being nice to one another", replies one woman.

"As a woman you have to follow Mary's way to go to Christ", says another passerby. (This comment no doubt confirms many viewers' worst suspicions about "Maryolatry".)

A man answers that he will go to heaven "by treating people properly. Be fair to everyone."

"I don't know. Just behaving myself", says another fellow, who admits he does not have a good answer.

An equally confused man replies, "By trying to live a clean and decent life, I guess."

Not one of these is a good answer, though each contains a partial truth (see Mt 19:16–17). These people are easy foils for Fundamentalists, and their confused ideas are allowed to stand for the Catholic position on salvation.

Footnotes in the transcript flesh out the on-screen arguments, but often disingenuously. In one scene the narrator claims that "Catholicism has continued to add new doctrines to the Catholic faith from the traditions of men. The belief that the nature of the bread changed at the Mass was not added to official doctrine until the Fourth Lateran Council in 1215. This was the first time the Church sanctioned the theory of transubstantiation." The footnote gives a lengthy quotation from *The New Catholic Encyclopedia*. The reader is left with the impression that the Real Presence was a doctrine "invented" shortly before the Fourth Lateran Council and that belief in the doctrine has been coterminous with the use of the term "transubstantiation". The transcript does not quote from the second paragraph of the encyclopedia's article on transubstantiation: "Although the term is neither biblical nor patristic, the idea it expresses is as old as Christian revelation. The scriptural evidence [five passages are cited] requires that the bread cease to exist and that Christ's body be made present." (The terms "Trinity" and "Incarnation" are not biblical either, but Fundamentalists have no qualms about using them.)

Further paragraphs in the encyclopedia demonstrate that the Fathers of the Church taught the Real Presence, even though the technical term "transubstantiation" was not used until the medieval period. Until that time there was no noticeable public denial of the Real Presence, but, when the problem spread beyond a few ivory-tower thinkers, the Fourth Lateran Council, in order to eliminate confusion on the subject, imposed a new theological term—but not a new doctrine. The doctrine came straight from the New Testament, but that is not the impression left by the video or its transcript.

This historical situation mirrors one that occurred in the fourth century. The heresy of Arianism taught that Jesus was not the God-man but only a man, though the best of all men. At the Council of Nicaea in 325 the bishops defined how the Son's nature is related to the Father's. The parties leaning toward the heretical position wanted to adopt the Greek term *homoiousios* ("like substance"), but the Council settled on *homoousios* ("same substance") because only that term—which is not found in the Bible—promised to preserve the truth that the Son is not merely like the Father (so are we, since we are made in the Father's image) but shares the Father's divine nature and is himself God.

The original release of *Catholicism: Crisis of Faith* showed a statue depicting a woman attached to a crucifix. The statue was said to be located in the cathedral in Quito, Ecuador. The narrator explained that Catholics have so confused the role of Mary in redemption, equating her work with her Son's, that they believe she too suffered for their sins. But the confusion was the video's. According to Bishop Antonio Arregui of Quito, the statue is not in the cathedral but in a monastery in Quito, and the woman depicted is not Mary but a local saint known as Santa Liberata, "she who received liberation". She is said to have been the daughter of a Portuguese prince. "Her father wished to marry her to a non-Christian and corrupt prince", explains Bishop Arregui. "When she refused, her father ordered that she be crucified." Historians have not precisely determined the woman's dates. Her feast is celebrated locally on July 20. When she appears without a cross, she is shown "with the arms extended and a bit raised. Sometimes she wears a royal crown. In some pictures there is someone at her feet playing an instrument, as if she were courted by a young man."

To McCarthy's credit, the scene with the statue was excised from the video. He says it was cut out as soon as the falsity of the representation was brought to his attention, but he admits it was still in the video almost two years after the initial release. The fact that such an outlandish claim—that Mary too was crucified—appeared in the original version at all tends to undercut McCarthy's comment that the video "was produced under the direction of former Catholics aware of Catholic sensitivities. Care was taken to avoid unnecessary offense."

Bill Jackson is the head of Christians Evangelizing Catholics, a Fundamentalist group engaging in the distribution of anti-papal literature. Raised a Protestant, Jackson "accepted Jesus" in 1949, then went to a Bible college in England. He began missionary work to the Irish people in 1957. In honor of his spending a third of a century evangelizing Catholics, he was given an honorary doctorate by Baptist College in Montana.

Jackson's ministry had been headquartered in Louisville, Kentucky. It was moved to Littleton, Colorado, a suburb of Denver, in part so it could coordinate the attempt to reach the hundreds of thousands of young Catholics expected to attend World Youth Day in Denver to see John Paul II. Jackson mailed out, apparently to Catholics as well as to Protestants, a card with a reproduction of the statue that appeared in the video's original release. An accompanying letter said,

> There are some Catholics who, while they know that Mary was not actually nailed to a cross, would think this to be a fitting reminder of what she suffered. . . . There are other Catholics who would be horrified to think that anywhere in the world there would be Catholic piety which could accept Mary on a crucifix. . . . There might be some of you who would think that, by printing such a card, we are just Protestants trying to "get at" Mary and Marian piety within the Catholic Church. Let me hasten to assure you that I have the highest regard for Mary, the mother of Jesus. . . . Your response to this message will be appreciated.

Catholics who came upon the cards wrote to Jackson. Perhaps their complaints to him were relayed to McCarthy and helped prompt him to yank the "crucified Mary" scene from the video.

Toward the end of *Catholicism: Crisis of Faith* is a snippet from the motion picture *Martin Luther*. The segment is introduced by the narrator, who says, "This conflict between Scripture and Tradition was at the heart of the Reformation during the Middle Ages." In the snippet the Catholic prosecutor is shown saying, "Dr. Luther, you admitted these writings were yours. Will you tell us now, do you persist in what you have written here, or are you prepared to retract these writings and the beliefs they contain?"

Luther replies, "I ask pardon if I lack the manners that befit this court. I was not brought up in kings' palaces, but in the seclusion of the cloister. I am asked to retract these writings . . ."

The narrator interrupts and asks rhetorically, "Protestant critics? Not exactly. The leaders of the Reformation were all Catholic priests and theologians." He then mentions John Wycliffe, John Hus, Huldreich Zwingli, Martin Luther, and, incorrectly, John Calvin, who never was a priest.

The brief segment from *Martin Luther* is credited as being produced by Lutheran Film Associates and used "courtesy of Gateway Films/Vision Video". Walter Jensen of Lutheran Film Associates confirmed that *Martin Luther* is in the public domain and so can be used by anyone; no permission is necessary. He said Lutheran Film Associates was not made aware that a portion of the film would be in McCarthy's video. Jensen noted that he was "concerned" about the use of the film by anti-Catholics.

William Curtis of Vision Video said that McCarthy's organization approached Vision Video for permission to use the film and that Vision Video "thought they would do a helpful critique" of modern Catholicism, but Curtis characterizes *Catholicism: Crisis of Faith* as "a Catholic basher". He said Vision Video was "very, very disappointed" with McCarthy's production, and in his estimation the video offers "a very biased presentation" of Catholicism. Lumen Productions hoped to have Vision Video distribute the video—Curtis said McCarthy sent his office review copies—but Vision Video "refused to distribute" the final product and was "rather disgusted" with its contents. Curtis said of the video and its contents that his company "would not endorse or support that at all".

One of the former priests featured in *Catholicism: Crisis of Faith* is Bob Bush. McCarthy's newsletter introduced Bush to its readers this way:

> Late on the night of March 17, St. Patrick's Day, 1981, a small press produced our first publication, a booklet entitled *Good News for Catholics*. The next day 800 of the 3,000 Catholics departing from a ceremony at a local civic auditorium received a free copy. Jesuit priest Bob Bush was in that crowd. He was searching for God, but he didn't receive a booklet. There simply were not enough. Five years later, Bob, having learned the gospel through his own Scripture studies, left the priesthood and the Roman Catholic Church. When he learned of the opportunity that had almost been his in 1981, he remarked, "That booklet could have saved me a couple of years!"

Bush's is the first voice heard in the video after the narrator's. The scene is the church at the Jesuit-run University of San Francisco. Bush looks into the camera and says, "This is St. Ignatius Church. It is adjacent to the University of San Francisco. I studied here during my years of seminary training. My name is Bob Bush. I was ordained here in 1966. Twenty-one years later I submitted my letter of resignation." This wording is so imprecise that viewers might conclude that Bush's entire theological training took place at USF. According to the registrar's office, Bush indeed studied at USF, but only during the summers of 1964, 1965, and 1966, and each summer he took only two courses, Spanish and theology. To the extent he learned Catholic theology, he learned most of it elsewhere.

Bush appears eight times in the video, each instance only a sound bite. After another former priest and a former nun

speak against the Immaculate Conception and its chief consequence, Mary's sinlessness, Bush sums up for the viewer:
" 'All have sinned and fallen short of the glory of God' [Rom
3:23]. All have fallen. Yet the Catholic Church defined that
Mary was conceived without sin." Bush demonstrates Fundamentalists' strength and weakness: simplicity and oversimplifi-
cation. The "proof" is simple, a single verse. It is quoted as
though it can be interpreted only univocally. The viewer is
led to a single conclusion: if everyone has sinned, Mary must
have sinned; if the Catholic Church teaches she was sinless,
she must be teaching erroneously. This is the simplicity of
the argument, and it is an argument that appeals immediately
to minds uncluttered with questions.

The simplicity that appeals to some people looks like over-
simplification to others. They think to themselves along these
lines: What does it mean to say "All have sinned"? It must
mean, and certainly Fundamentalists mean by it, that all
people have committed actual sins, sins that are their own
acts, as distinguished from original sin, the stain of which is
inherited by us from our first parents, who sinned at the
origin of the race. Is the sentence "All have sinned" to be
taken broadly or with implied exceptions? Apparently the
latter, since everyone knows that neither children below the
age of reason nor people born severely retarded are capable
of sin. Thus Paul could not have been referring to either
young children or the severely retarded in Romans 3:23 because they have not sinned. To whom was he referring? No
doubt to the adult recipients of his letter. If his words allowed
for obvious exceptions, could it not be that he allowed for
another, unmentioned exception—Mary?

That is the kind of thinking someone not given to over-
simplification would engage in. It is not the kind of thinking
anti-Catholics appearing in this video engage in. The sound

bites in which their thoughts are presented are arguments that they themselves find convincing, and those sound bites contain no nuances. This is certainly the case with one of the former priests interviewed, Bart Brewer, head of Mission to Catholics International. His autobiography, *Pilgrimage from Rome*, is featured in the catalogue distributed by McCarthy's ministry. Brewer, like Bob Bush, speaks eight times in the video. The first time he says, "The Roman Catholic Church teaches that the Mass is a propitiatory sacrifice, which means that it appeases the wrath of God, that indeed it does take away sins. However, the Scripture is very clear about the fact that there is only one propitiatory sacrifice, namely, what our Lord did on the cross." Here he leaves the issue, much as he leaves it in his tracts, his newsletter, and his autobiography. Brewer appears unwilling to attempt to counter his opponents' natural and frequently stated rejoinder, that the Mass is not a new sacrifice but is a re-presentation of the same sacrifice as on Calvary.

This is not mere wordplay. It is easy enough to see how the Mass might be a new sacrifice that only mimics Calvary. It takes a little more effort, but not much, to entertain the possibility that somehow God permits that once-in-history sacrifice to become really present in a different (sacramental rather than historical) way on Catholic altars. This possibility deserves consideration. If it is untrue, it deserves to be refuted on its own merits. If it is impossible for God to arrange such a re-presentation, that impossibility needs to be demonstrated. A thorough critic or scholar would not dismiss cavalierly the Catholic position the way Brewer does—and a cavalier attitude is unmistakable throughout *Catholicism: Crisis of Faith*.

Back to Bob Bush. When the Catholic understanding of salvation is discussed, Bush brings up purgatory. "But when you search through the Scriptures, you go all the way through, you know, through Genesis, Exodus, Leviticus, all the way down to the Book of Revelation, you go all the way through, and you won't find it. There is no purgatory in there." Not by name, maybe, but it is there. After his death, Jesus "went to preach to the spirits in prison" (1 Pet 3:19). What was this place or state? In Catholic literature it is called by various names, but it well may have been purgatory. In any case, it was a third state, neither heaven (which was not opened until the Resurrection) nor hell (because the spirits Jesus preached to were not damned).

Then there is Revelation 21:27, which says that "nothing unclean" will enter heaven. This is a key verse. Most Fundamentalists would accept Martin Luther's idea of forensic justification: Christians are declared by God to be righteous but are not, by that declaration, made righteous. They are, so to speak, still dirty but are covered with a white cloak through Christ's merits. They look clean but are not. If all this were true, then all Christians die unclean because their souls have not been made clean but only declared to be clean. What follows is that, if Revelation 21:27 is applied, these Christians would be unable to enter heaven. Naturally, Fundamentalists will not put up with such a conclusion, even if it is a logical consequence of their own principles, but neither Fundamentalists in general nor Bob Bush in particular will tackle this problem, which might seem to them to have no solution. Yet there is a solution, and that solution is purgatory, through which souls are made clean.

Aside from the narrator, the anti-Catholic with the most lines in the video is Frank Eberhardt, who studied for the priesthood at Saint Joseph Seminary in Kingston, New Jersey. Eberhardt appears on screen right after Richard Chilson runs his hand across his head and leaves an impression of confusion. "The Catholic priest cannot really explain how that the finished work of Christ on the cross is continued today in the Mass." In fact Chilson did explain it, but his explanation was left on the cutting room floor—a fact Eberhardt does not mention. Nor does he mention that he puts words into Catholic mouths.

At one point the narrator interviews two Catholic women on the street. One says she does not believe in purgatory. "I think of it as an outdated idea. I don't know what it means." (It is not clear how she can reject a doctrine she cannot even define.) The other woman says about purgatory, "I have very mixed feelings on that. I am not awfully sure." She seems no better grounded in her faith than the first woman. Each is a walking stereotype. The narrator asks rhetorically whether we "earn" salvation. Then comes a cut to Eberhardt. "The problem with that, of course, is that the Scripture nowhere says that we can pay for our own sins." He speaks a few more sentences, but none of them tells the viewer that the Catholic Church does not teach that we "pay for our own sins". Eberhardt does not quote any Catholic authority on the issue, for the simple reason, of course, that every Catholic authority—every pope, council, and theologian that has considered the issue—condemns the idea that we earn salvation. The Catholic position is that salvation is a gift from God, and you cannot earn a gift. Either Eberhardt, despite all his training while a Catholic, never grasped this elementary fact, or he willingly obscures it today, the better to make a case against the Catholic Church.

Victor Alfonso is another ex-Jesuit. He first pops up right after Doreen D'Antonio, a former Sister of Christian Charity, explains that in her convent there was a statue of a saint for every need: "If we lost something we would pray to St. Anthony. . . . St. Blaise if we had a sore throat. . . . We had an elevator for older nuns, and in that elevator was this humongous medal of St. Christopher. It was amazing. We would have little statues of Mary and Joseph. . . . We would have the little statue right on the window sill, hoping and praying that statue would prevent it from raining on a particular day." D'Antonio does not broach the possibility that the nuns she lived with were not really superstitious or that maybe she was but they were not. Perhaps she read into their sentimental piety more than was there and is retrojecting into their minds her own misconceptions. We never find out.

The video moves straight to Alfonso, who quotes Exodus 20:4, which concerns making idols for worship, and the narrator interrupts to note that Alfonso "served as a Jesuit priest for twenty-one years". Alfonso says, " 'You shall not bow down to them' or worship them [Ex 20:5]. It's the same word." He means that to kneel before a statue necessarily must be to worship the statue. He appears oblivious to a natural conclusion drawn from his own (erroneous) premises: The fervent Fundamentalist who clutches his Bible to his breast while kneeling in prayer must be worshiping a book. After all, books, like statues, are made by human hands and might become idols when used for religious purposes.

Then the narrator alleges that the Catholic Church "regularly omits" the injunction against idol worship from her listing of the Ten Commandments in catechisms. Alfonso claims that the Church dropped what Protestants call the Second Commandment and, in order to end up with a total of ten, split the final Commandment into two parts, making the Ninth and Tenth Commandments. "So they had the Ten Commandments. Now this is crookery. This is trickery. You've changed the Commandments. But why did you drop the Second Commandment? Because there is a lot of business in making statues."

In the transcript of the video there is a footnote to the narrator's charge that the Church "regularly omits" Exodus 20:4 from the listing of the Ten Commandments: "Instead, the Church considers it part of the First Commandment." Here, in the video's own transcript, is a clue to the answer to Alfonso. In the Bible the Commandments are not numbered. How best to split up the verses so we end up with Ten Commandments? The Catholic view is that what Protestants call the First and Second Commandments really deal with the same thing, idolatry, so they should be merged into one Commandment. What Protestants call the Tenth Commandment really deals with two different things, adultery (coveting your neighbor's wife) and envy (coveting your neighbor's goods), so the Catholic Church lists these separately. This makes good sense, but Alfonso, if he knows the reasoning, keeps it to himself.

Another former Catholic appearing repeatedly is Wilma Sullivan, who joined the Sisters of Mercy of the Union in 1967. Her formal journey out of the Church began in 1973, when she began to be proselytized by a woman she had met in a hospital while undergoing minor surgery. Her disaffection with Catholicism had begun earlier, and, as in so many cases, it began with the Real Presence. "My faith crisis began at Communion. The priest held the host in front of me and said, 'The body of Christ.' Before I could say the expected response, 'Amen,' a thought went through my mind for the first time: 'Is it really?'" Sullivan unknowingly recapitulates the story given in John 6. After miraculously multiplying loaves and fish, Jesus promised that he would provide his followers, miraculously, not food for their bodies but food for their souls. He tells them this food will be his own flesh and blood (Jn 6:51–58). The Jews who are listening on the periphery of the crowd take Jesus literally and ask, "How can this man give us his flesh to eat?" (Jn 6:53). Jesus does not correct them. He does not say they are wrongly taking a symbol in a literalistic sense. He reemphasizes what he has just said, insisting that there can be no spiritual life within his followers unless they eat his flesh and drink his blood (Jn 6:54). Jesus repeats himself, and then some of his disciples revolt. "This is a hard saying. Who can listen to it?" (Jn 6:61), they asked, and they "no longer went about with him" (Jn 6:66). This is the only place in the New Testament in which it is recorded that any of his disciples abandoned Jesus for a doctrinal reason. Instead of calling after them, explaining that he was speaking metaphorically, he let them go. There was no need to correct their misinterpretation because they had not misinterpreted him.

In this episode is a telling verse overlooked by many. In verse 64 Judas falls away. Unlike the other disciples who could not accept the Real Presence, he did not have the courage of his convictions. They walked away from Jesus; Judas fell away in his heart and mind but stayed at Jesus' side. Later he would become a thief, stealing from the common purse, and a betrayer, but here is his first great betrayal. It is a betrayal copied by millions throughout history, Wilma Sullivan being one of them. For reasons probably unknown even to herself, she discards the key doctrine enunciated in John 6: "Is it really?" From there the road to apostasy is direct and swift.

The newsletter published by Good News for Catholics includes letters. A Protestant pastor in Texas writes, "We showed *Catholicism: Crisis of Faith* the other night to our whole congregation. Before I showed the film to the congregation, I asked for a show of hands of who had been born and raised Catholic. I was surprised to see at least fifty percent had been. The response [to the video] was overwhelming. I was especially moved, having been myself born and raised Catholic. I left the Catholic faith about sixteen years ago. . . . I attempted also at first to both serve and change the Catholic Church. . . . I finally realized the effort to be futile."

Another letter informs us that a one-time Catholic in New York "recently attended a funeral for a member of our church. Though a believer and member of our Evangelical church, her family thought it best for her funeral to take place in the Roman Catholic Church." *Catholicism: Crisis of Faith* was used to instruct the members of the writer's own church on what they could expect to find at the Catholic parish. They took advantage of the situation: "The truth was preached in love to her family. They were very moved, and three members of her family have begun to attend our church."

Another correspondent explains that his "brother-in-law was saved out of an Italian/Irish Catholic family. . . . I gave them the video, and he showed it to his Catholic parents. This viewing was followed by the best discussions which they have had. His dad borrowed the tape and invited priests from a number of parishes over to see it!" The response from the priests is not given. Perhaps some of them had devastating rejoinders to the charges made in the video. More likely they pooh-poohed it, as though that would take care of this display of anti-Catholicism. It does not.

If clear thinking and balanced presentations of opposing views were the norm, anti-Catholicism in the form shown in *Catholicism: Crisis of Faith* would have died out long ago. This video never would have been produced or, if produced, never would have had an impact. But it has had an impact, large or small, because most Catholics remain untrained in the defense of their faith. The video's power comes, not from its arguments, but from the lack of any organized opposition to them. When it convinces, it convinces by default. If it were paired with a Catholic video, audiences seeing both at one sitting would move in only one direction, toward Rome. Until such a Catholic video is produced, the home team will be playing catch-up.

26

Three against One

Although the incident happened some years ago, it remains instructive and worth recalling. It was the first opportunity many Fundamentalists had to hear a defense of the Catholic religion. John Ankerberg, a leading televangelist, hosted a seven-part series on Catholicism. His guests were Walter Martin, head of the Christian Research Institute, and Mitch Pacwa, a Jesuit then teaching at Loyola University in Chicago and now at the University of Dallas. Since many Catholics watched *The John Ankerberg Show* regularly, and since many more learned of the series through word of mouth, this was no small event even for Catholics. Not often is our side given a chance to put its position before viewers. When Fundamentalist ministers rail against "Romanism" on television, they do not have a "Romanist" on stage to correct them. When radio evangelists present skewed interpretations of Catholicism, no one is there to set the record straight. So this was no insignificant series.

Wanting to find out more about the origin and conduct of the series, I phoned Pacwa. I began by asking whether the whole of the discussion was aired. No, he said. He and Martin talked about "call no man your father" (Mt 23:9), and that twelve-minute segment was dropped, as was a comparably long portion of their discussion of the papacy. Many smaller segments never made it out of the editing room—segments in which Pacwa felt he did particularly well.

I said to him that this was not a one-on-one debate; it was almost three-on-one. On one side, Mitch Pacwa. On the other, Walter Martin, plus moderator John Ankerberg—who was no neutral observer but an active debater on the Protestant side and who, in some of the seven shows, spoke as many as a third of the lines—plus the announcer, who usually gave a fair (though much too long) discussion of the differences between the Catholic and Protestant positions and who, in doing so, usually gave extra emphasis to the latter.

"Were you taken by surprise? Did they pull a fast one?"

In a way, said Pacwa. The seven programs were filmed at one sitting. The principals were before the cameras from 7:00 P.M. to midnight. There was no chance for Pacwa to think at leisure about the format of the first program and to insist on changes in later programs. He had to take what was offered. (I might say I have had to learn the same way: being bushwhacked at a debate is at least educative, and now I am careful to work out the ground rules in detail.)

"Were you familiar with *The John Ankerberg Show* before this? Did you know its format?"

"Not at all", said Pacwa. He did not know what to expect. Frequent viewers later told him they never saw Ankerberg so "involved" in what was supposed to be a one-on-one debate. Apparently he usually acts more like a true moderator.

"How did the Ankerberg people select you?"

"They originally had asked another priest, but his schedule was so full he was unable to accept. He gave them my name."

Ankerberg's representatives were especially interested in Pacwa's orthodoxy. Was he a *real* Catholic or merely a cultural Catholic? They did not want someone who, in the clutch, would say, "Oh, we don't believe *that* any longer—

Vatican II changed all that." Most Fundamentalists know Vatican II did not change any doctrines, even if some Catholics like to imagine it did, and Ankerberg's people wanted someone who would not substitute his private prejudices for official beliefs. Pacwa satisfied them on that score. (He is so solid that he did not hesitate to tell me that he had been saying rosaries and novenas for Walter Martin's conversion. How many priests would bother to do that? Martin was raised in the Episcopal Church but attended Catholic schools as a boy, and he fancied himself an authority on things Roman. He was best known for a book on cults and, unlike many other Fundamentalists, did not classify Catholicism as a cult. Pacwa became a friend of the Martin family. Martin died a few years after the taping.)

Pacwa also satisfied Ankerberg's representatives in having experience in speaking in public. First of all, he was a professor. He "grew up a greaser" in Chicago and earned his Ph.D. at Vanderbilt ("a hot-bed of anti-Catholicism"), where he majored in the Old Testament and minored in the New. Some years ago Catholic laymen asked him to host a call-in radio program. He did, and it aired five times a week for two months—until the money ran out. That got him an invitation to appear on a Protestant television program, and that brought him to the attention of Mother Angelica, head of the Eternal Word Television Network. Pacwa has taped scores of episodes for her on biblical, doctrinal, and spiritual topics.

"Was there an agreed-upon format for the Ankerberg series?" I asked.

"Not really", said Pacwa. "I was just told there would be a debate format and that we'd discuss Mary, the papacy, justification, and so on." He did not know much about Ankerberg or Martin beforehand, and he said the announcer's voice-over comments were edited in later, so until he saw the series he had no idea how little on-air time he actually got. I told him my count of lines in the transcript indicated he spoke less than 30 percent of the total lines, and, since most of his lines were short, he probably got less than a quarter of the air time.

"What was your goal in going on the air?"

"These people have a warped view of what we teach", said Pacwa. "They want us to be crypto-Pelagians. They want to think we believe salvation is entirely by our own efforts."

He remarked that at the taping a Seventh-Day Adventist minister was in the audience. (The Seventh-Day Adventist Church has been, historically, highly anti-Catholic.) The man, in his seventies, approached Pacwa and said, "What I was taught about Catholics was contrary to what you really believe." He apologized and explained that he was writing a book on religion. The Jesuit suggested several Catholic titles he should read first. I noted to Pacwa that this demonstrated the value of debates, even "set-ups". Fundamentalists often are astounded at how much of what they "know" about Catholicism just is not so.

"Why do Fundamentalists have such an interest in the Catholic Church?" I asked. "We don't find any Fundamentalists organizing to oppose Anglicanism or Methodism or Eastern Orthodoxy."

"Other churches are not seen as a threat. It's partly a matter of numbers. Mainline Protestant churches are declining in membership. We're gaining, even if modestly in this country. Then there are the myths about the Church. They spark interest."

"What do you see as the origin of the Fundamentalist problem?"

"I think the attitude toward justification is absolutely essential", said Pacwa. "As you know, many Catholics want a closer relationship with Christ, but they *don't* hear about it in church. Fundamentalists talk about it, and the contrast draws Catholics to Fundamentalism. What's more, many Fundamentalists have more faith than some of our priests. A lot of clergy don't take orthodoxy seriously, and a lot of priests don't know anything about apologetics." They could not discuss religion with Fundamentalists even if they wanted to.

"How should we approach Fundamentalists?"

"First, the Catholic must spend time praying for the person to be approached—this is a *sine qua non*. Prayer helps to avoid bitterness. Then the Catholic must learn his own faith. He must listen to what the Fundamentalist's questions really mean. Remember, these people are honest and sincere, and they're trying to save us from going to hell. Our approach to them must be scripturally based—abstract reasoning and historical analysis have little influence in Protestantism."

During the seven shows—all taped in one evening—there aired pitches for "Offer R-2". By sending in thirty dollars, viewers could receive a transcript of all programs plus a book titled *Roman Catholicism*. The book was not the one by Loraine Boettner; the author was Richard Knolls. Boettner's identically titled and better-known book is mentioned in the footnotes, though.

The transcript is what one might expect, but the book must have been, at first glance, a disappointment to many, since it was not typeset but typewritten. Not a narrative, it was an extended outline. Still, at somewhat more than two hundred pages, it is a more ambitious work than most Fundamentalist writers are inclined to put out, even those who are "professional anti-Catholics".

The first thing one noticed about *The John Ankerberg Show*, or, at least, about the series on Catholicism, was the annoying background music, which was too fast-paced for a serious discussion. It was not wholly inappropriate, perhaps, but hardly what one would expect, just as one would not expect ragtime as a replacement for Elgar at graduation exercises. If the music was questionable, so were the titles for the guests. On the screen the Catholic was labeled "Fr. Mitchell Pacwa, S.J., representing Roman Catholicism". The Protestant was labeled "Dr. Walter Martin, representing Orthodox Christianity"—a subtle jab. Martin wore a pectoral cross (without a corpus, naturally), something generally reserved for "popish" ecclesiastics. This may have been a sentimental hold-over from his early Catholic schooling. While Fundamentalists do not object to the cross as a symbol, they usually do not like to sport it in a "Catholic" manner. On bumper stickers, yes; in the style of John Paul II, no. It is said that at times Martin's wording betrayed his background, and it is certainly true that he was more open to Catholicism than are most Fundamentalists who speak about it in public. Though his mind seemed made up, it probably was not closed.

Most Catholics who have heard of John Ankerberg know his name only because it was he who leveled the most serious charges in the PTL (Praise The Lord) scandal involving Jim and Tammy Bakker. But not a few Catholics know him from *The John Ankerberg Show*, which then was broadcast nationwide. For years he was one of the top television evangelists, even if his name usually was not mentioned in the same breath as those of Jerry Falwell, Jimmy Swaggart, Oral Roberts, and Pat Robertson. At the time of the broadcasts, his ministry, headquartered in Chattanooga, Tennessee, distributed a brochure explaining that he was a Baptist minister who had received his bachelor's degree from the University of Illinois and who had done graduate work at Trinity Seminary and Bethel Theological Seminary. "He has spoken on nearly 80 college and university campuses in the United States and has also addressed large audiences and mass meetings in Africa, Asia, and North and South America." He was called "an experienced speaker and defender of the faith".

The John Ankerberg Show was a half-hour program airing weekly. "Our television audience is able to hear the evidence for the truth claims of those representing non-Christian beliefs and compare it with the evidence for the truth claims of those holding to biblical Christianity. Non-Christian guests are invited to present their position and discuss its merits and supporting evidence in face-to-face discussion with Christian guests whose views and claims differ." In this approach Ankerberg's show differed from those of his better-known colleagues. They usually featured only committed Protestants, but he opened his studio to people opposed to his position. His brochure noted that "we do not try to represent the non-Christian's position. Rather, we invite the best non-Christian spokesmen available to come and speak. We are totally fair in letting them state their case." (Yes, but "fair" should not be interpreted to mean "equal time", as Pacwa discovered.)

The brochure included a comment from a viewer: "Dear Sir: Even when Mr. Ankerberg is 100 percent right, out of fairness which should transcend all beliefs, he should remain a referee and never side with any view. If he cannot do this, then he should discontinue his role on the program." Ankerberg answered by saying that "nobody is neutral", which is true enough. He said his "questions are intended to keep the conversation on track", and, if the series with Pacwa was any indication, that is what he did. Still, Catholic viewers could not be faulted for thinking Ankerberg was as much a debate opponent for Pacwa as was Walter Martin. He should have let Martin carry the Protestant side, interrupting only to keep the other two from straying from the topic or from being too long-winded. However that may be, at least Ankerberg devoted several programs to Catholicism, which is more than can be said for other television evangelists, and he took pains to present the Catholic side as it really is. In that he did a service to his viewers.

Walter Martin, a Fundamentalist writer best known for his book *The Kingdom of the Cults*, founded and headed the California-based Christian Research Institute and hosted a popular radio program, *The Bible Answer Man*, carried throughout the country. Among Fundamentalists, Martin was considered an authority on Catholicism. He did not dispute that assessment. In the first program of the series, he said, "What we're really talking about are differences that persist since Vatican II between classic Roman Catholic theology and Protestant theology or Reformation theology. . . . I'm [as] well acquainted with [these subjects] as any scholar in the area would be."

The first program concerned the papacy, and the discussion was continued on the subsequent program. After Pacwa pointed out that it was the Church, through her popes, bishops, and councils, that decided what constitutes the canon of the New Testament, Martin attempted to demonstrate that papal authority is unreliable because there has been a long succession of papal errors. "In Vatican I," he said, "which was the cornerstone of all the power of the contemporary papacy, [papal infallibility] was clearly defined for the first time in history. . . . Now, when that was done at Vatican I on July 13, 1870, an argument was raised on the floor, voted on by eighteen bishops supporting it, and this is what was stated, historically, if I may quote it: 'Well, venerable brethren, history raises its voice to assure us that popes have erred. You may protest against it or deny it as you please, I'll prove it.'" Martin then read at length from a speech allegedly given at

Vatican I. He did not identify the speaker, except to say he was an archbishop. The portion of the speech Martin quoted consisted of short accusations against more than a dozen popes—for instance, "Honorius adhered to Monothelitism", and "Sixtus V published an edition of the Bible and by a bull recommended it to be read. Pius VII condemned the reading of it."

Some of the charges, including the two reproduced here, are groundless. Honorius was not an adherent to Monothelitism, the heresy that held that in Christ there was only one will, the divine. (The orthodox position, held by both Catholics and Protestants, is that he had two wills, the divine and the human, and they were in perfect union.) In fact, Honorius got into trouble by deciding to take no stand. Honorius' fault was that he chose to remain silent and not issue a teaching at all. That means that the Honorius case had nothing to do with an exercise of papal infallibility. Neither did the case involving Sixtus V and Pius VII. The former approved for use an edition of the Vulgate Bible. After errors were discovered in the editing, the latter withdrew permission to use it. Again, no exercise of papal infallibility. Popes are not infallible when they decide for or against the use of a particular edition of the Bible. Their infallibility extends only to matters of faith and morals, and weighing the merits of a particular translation of the Bible falls into neither category. It is a matter of discipline, not belief.

These are just two of many "papal errors" brought up by Martin through the reading of the speech said to have been given at Vatican I. As one who prides himself on his familiarity with Catholic doctrines, he should have had a better understanding of when, according to the Church, infallibility applies and when it does not. Infallibility cannot be disproved by referring to cases that do not fall within the Church's

definition of the charism. The way to disprove papal infallibility is to find errors that arose while popes claimed to be
exercising their infallibility. If Martin had shown that, he
would have been on to something, but not one of his examples qualified. Either they were factually wrong—such as
attributing a false teaching to a pope who never taught it—or
they were inapplicable—showing some change in disciplin-
ary policy from one pope to another but no change in an
official definition of faith or morals. As Pacwa explained,
"The pope's infallibility does not mean that the pope is right
all the time. In no way does the Catholic Church even teach
that. He's infallible only when he speaks *ex cathedra*. . . . He
has to say that explicitly to be speaking infallibly. Secondly, it
has to be to the whole Church, not to one part or one
individual of the Church, but to everybody in the Church.
And thirdly, it has to be on the issue of faith and morals. He
cannot infallibly say that the stock market will drop."

If Martin had been "up" on Catholicism, if he had done
his homework, he would have appreciated the distinctions.
What is more, he never would have made use of the speech
in the first place, not just because it was doctrinally wrong,
which it is, but because it was never given at Vatican I. The
speech is a well-known forgery.

The "archbishop" who supposedly gave the speech, and
who was not identified by Martin, was Josef Strossmayer,
ordinary of Diakovar in Croatia. (He actually was a bishop,
not an archbishop.) Strossmayer indeed opposed the promulgation of the doctrine of papal infallibility, but not because
he disbelieved in it. He was a staunch nationalist in a region
torn by religious strife. His major concern was the conflict
between Catholics and Eastern Orthodox. He believed there
was a real possibility that corporate reunion between Catholicism and Orthodoxy could be realized, but he knew

the Orthodox were skittish. Their break from unity, occurring centuries earlier, had been more political than doctrinal, and Strossmayer thought they were close to being wooed back—and could be, so long as no stumbling blocks were thrown in their way. He saw the doctrine of papal infallibility as such a stumbling block. (John Henry Newman, by 1870 long a Catholic, also opposed the promulgation of the doctrine, for similar reasons, but he too believed in the pope's infallibility.)

Strossmayer spoke against the proposed schema at the council, but he did not deliver the speech from which Martin read. That speech was drafted by an ex-Augustinian monk who had left the Church in bitterness, and Strossmayer's name was stuck on it. A close reading of the speech demonstrates that its author was not what one would call historically or theologically literate. Such a thing could not be said about Strossmayer. A university professor, he was highly educated, and Pius IX praised him on his elegant Latin—this at a time when it was a matter of course for bishops to be fluent in Latin. Strossmayer was a stand-out among well-educated ecclesiastics.

The speech, particularly its early parts, which were not quoted by Martin, betrays its author as a Protestant. The wording is wrong. It suggests, for instance, that "Strossmayer" only shortly before the council read through the New Testament for the first time and discovered no hint of the papacy. That is hardly to be expected from a theology professor, who, one might think, would have been familiar with Scripture. No, there is no doubt the speech was a forgery, and it has long been recognized as such, at least in Catholic circles. Where did Martin find it? He did not say, but he may have taken it from the appendix to Henry T. Hudson's *Papal Power*. There the speech was given in full and attributed to Strossmayer. (This is particularly ironic since the main charge in Hudson's book was that the papacy gained its temporal and religious power through the adroit use of forgeries, such as the Donation of Constantine. Here was a debunker of forgeries passing one off as genuine!)

If Martin had been as well trained in things Catholic as he imagined, he should have known the speech was a forgery. Think of it this way. Let us say you read a tract that claims that Jerry Falwell has asserted that, yes, John Paul II is the legitimate successor to Peter and that Christ appointed Peter the first pope. Startling news, eh? It might occur to you that, given what you know about Falwell, there might be a few misprints floating around. After all, such an acknowledgment would be out of character for him. You would not expect a leading non-Catholic to support the papacy's claims. So what would you do? You would do some homework. You would try to track down the source of the tract's information, or you might write to Falwell and ask him if the tract is accurate. At least, you should become suspicious. Martin evidently never was. He did not think this "archbishop's" comments were extraordinary, except that they supported his views. Had he been so inclined, he could have checked easily enough. Had he turned to the *Catholic Encyclopedia*, he would have found an article on Strossmayer, and he would have learned that the speech was a forgery. He would have seen references to further information about Strossmayer, and he could have checked those and the proceedings of Vatican I. Martin did none of this. (If he did, but still tried to pass off the speech as legitimate, then he was guilty of something worse than sloppiness.) What did this say about his credentials? Did it show he was as "well acquainted with [Catholicism] as any scholar in the area would be"?

The exchanges on *The John Ankerberg Show* are difficult to

summarize and difficult to recount. By its nature, a talk show is discursive. The participants wander from one point to another, interrupt one another regularly, and seldom are given enough time to state their positions clearly. Unlike a formal debate, for which the parties can prepare by composing written statements that will be read, on a talk show things are said off the top of one's head, which makes for a certain looseness. It also makes for some revealing comments.

The last program of the first series had as its topic the Virgin Mary. As might be anticipated, the discussion turned to Mary's status as mediatrix. Martin did not approve of the Catholic doctrine in the least, and he referred to the standard verse: "For there is one God, and one mediator between God and men, the man Christ Jesus" (1 Tim 2:5). Most Fundamentalists will admit only the narrowest interpretation of this sentence, concluding that if Christ is the sole mediator, no one else can participate in his mediation. Martin, at least, acknowledged an obvious exception, one that all Fundamentalists would acknowledge if only they looked at the matter at arm's length. He referred to "prayer that we can offer on earth for each other". If A prays to God for B, A is acting as a mediator. He is a go-between, and that is all a mediator is. While Martin admitted the obvious, that 1 Timothy 2:5 cannot be taken in the narrowest sense (though he did not frame his admission in so many words), he would not go so far as to say Mary could participate in mediatorship also. We can pray for one another here below, but she cannot pray for us in heaven.

"Well, again, so say you", answered Pacwa.

"But so says the New Testament", replied Martin.

"No, the New Testament doesn't say that. You assume that the New Testament means that."

"That's an argument from silence."

"Exactly—which you are also making!"

This short exchange may not make the point clear, so let us rephrase it. Martin said Mary cannot be a mediatrix because the Bible does not say she is a mediatrix. Pacwa noted that since the Bible is silent on the matter, neither affirming nor denying the issue explicitly, we cannot resolve the matter merely by pointing to a single verse, the way we can with some other doctrinal questions, such as the institution of the papacy, the historicity of the Resurrection, the fact of the Ascension—all of which are plainly mentioned in Scripture.

Martin went on to dangerous ground. His underlying principle, apparently, was that we are to keep to no doctrine or practice unless it is found on the face of Scripture. If that is the way we decide what to believe, how to act, then Fundamentalists themselves have problems. They would have, for example, no warrant for holding corporate worship on Sunday instead of Saturday. It was the Catholic Church that changed the day in post–New Testament times. To see how unhelpful the New Testament is, when taken alone, consider the Seventh-Day Adventists, who, looking solely at the Bible, say worship should be on Saturday, not Sunday. Another example: on Martin's principles, Fundamentalists would not believe in the Trinity as it is understood today. Cardinal Newman noted that the divinity of the Holy Spirit is not clear from the New Testament. It was, again, the Church that specified the content of trinitarian doctrine.

Pacwa pointed out, quite reasonably, that, while the New Testament may be silent on Mary's status as mediatrix, it is not silent on the angels' status. Revelation refers to their taking our prayers, like incense, before the throne of God. If they take our prayers to God, they first must have received the prayers from us. How? By our praying to them. There is no other way. Case closed—or, at least, it should have been

closed. The seven debates may not have changed many viewers' minds, but they probably modified some anti-Catholic
prejudices, and sometimes that is all the Catholic participant
asks for. A seed is planted, and the Holy Spirit takes care of
its nurture.

INDEX

Abraham, 91–93, 97
Acts (Scripture), 127
Adventism, 28, 110–18, 176
Airy, George Biddell, 57
Alfonso, Victor, 167–69
Ankerberg, John, 173–85
anti-intellectualism, 15, 36, 83–
  89
Antichrist, 91, 94, 97, 116
Arian heresy, 159
Arregui, Antonio, 160

Babylon, 59, 96, 146–48
Bakker, Jim, 105, 178
baptism, 69, 80–82
beast verses, 106, 110–16
  See also Antichrist
bells, 72–73
Benson, Robert Hugh, 140
Berry, Charles Allen, 140–48
Berthier, Louis-Alexandre,
  116
Bible
  beast verses, 106, 110–16
  brethren verses, 15, 44–46
  interpretation, 44–46, 84–89,
    129
  prophecies, 90–94, 95–98,
    107, 111–12
  proving truth of, 54–62

as sole rule of faith, 28, 34–
  35, 47–53, 139, 152
translations, 54, 85–89, 181
  See also specific books
Bible Answer Man, The (radio
  program), 180
bibliolatry, 89
  See also idolatry
Boettner, Loraine, 140, 177
Bones of Saint Peter, The
  (Walsh), 143–48
brethren verses, 15, 44–46
Brewer, Bartholomew, 19, 156,
  165
Bush, Bob, 163, 166

calendars, 90–94, 95–98
Calvin, John, 162
Canon Law, Code of, 69
Catholic Christianity (Chilson),
  154
Catholicism
  customs, 42, 68–75, 80–82,
    158–59, 168–69
  reasons for responding to
    anti-Catholicism, 9–17,
    20, 82–83, 130, 171
  and Sunday observance, 114–
    15, 186
  See also papacy; popes